COACHING
MATTERS

JOELLEN KILLION,

CINDY HARRISON,

CHRIS BRYAN, and

HEATHER CLIFTON

Learning Forward
504 S. Locust St.
Oxford, OH 45056
513-523-6029
800-727-7288
Fax: 513-523-0638
Email: office@learningforward.org
www.learningforward.org

COACHING MATTERS

By Joellen Killion, Cindy Harrison, Chris Bryan, and Heather Clifton

Editor & production: Valerie von Frank
Cover designer: Kitty Black

Printed in the United States of America
Item #B542
ISBN 978-1-936630-05-9

Dedication

Collectively, we have had the opportunity to work with thousands of coaches in hundreds of school systems throughout North America and beyond. We have witnessed these coaches strive to make a difference, to engage teachers and principals in the messy work of increasing student achievement, and to provide equitable opportunities for every student to learn. Coaches' work is challenging, and they have significant, visible accountability for student success.

To all of the coaches who have been our teachers, to the district office staff who are their champions, and to the principals who support them in their daily work, we extend our deepest appreciation for making a difference for so many students each day and for the teachers entrusted with those students' academic, social, emotional, and physical well-being.

This book is dedicated to you.

Table of contents

Preface

This book is about coaching — and ways to strengthen the practice and results of coaching. The authors offer guidance for those who are coaches and for those who support, serve, and supervise coaches by highlighting the main factors that influence coaching success.

This book also is about the more foundational question of whether coaching matters. In other words, does it work? After being in schools, observing and coaching coaches, and seeing firsthand how increased support for the complex act of teaching increases teacher effectiveness and student learning, the authors reply, unequivocally, yes. We have seen that coaching has tremendous potential to transform teaching and learning.

Yet we add that coaching makes a difference *if* the conditions, structures, and supports described in this book are either in place or are the focus of ongoing improvement work. The ingredients for successful coaching are neither magic nor mysterious. They are essentially the same ingredients included in nearly all effective school reform efforts: strong leadership, a clear focus and goals, essential resources, well-prepared staff, ongoing measures of assuring and monitoring progress, and rigorous evaluations.

This book incorporates what we have experienced firsthand and what research confirms about coaching. We have worked with coaches to prepare and support them in their work, with principals to help them understand how to engage successfully in a coaching effort, and with district and state leaders who implement coaching programs.

We recognize that there are multiple approaches or schools of thought related to coaching and multiple skill sets, training, and development programs designed to prepare coaches to support their clients. Many skillful experts are prepared to support coaching. Each approach, training, and expert adds knowledge and value to the field about coaching. We do not seek to advocate one approach over another but rather to establish this premise: Coaching matters in improving student and teacher learning if the coaching program and the coaches meet certain standards.

So, in this book, we describe the characteristics that distinguish effective coaching programs and those that affect teaching practices, student achievement, and school culture. We describe the practices that lead to results for teachers and students, describe responsibilities, and offer strategies for individual coaches, principals, and school systems to build a stronger coaching program.

Each chapter addresses a topic we believe is vitally important to coaching's success. Each is accompanied by tools, including extended readings, resources to use with teachers, strategies for accomplishing the work, and examples from coaches and school systems. We hope these tools will give coaches and system leaders who champion coaching a start in building their own tools that are more closely aligned with their individual programs.

This book, then, is for coaches, principals, and district leaders either beginning or retooling a coaching program. Leaders may revisit the topics for ongoing guidance to continually tune their programs.

Like yeast to bread, the conditions described within this book influence coaching's success — and its potential to transform student learning within schools.

Changing
standards

E ducators are facing an accelerating pace of change. The last three decades have been marked by intensifying scrutiny, calls for accountability, and remarkable shifts in teachers' roles. The significant changes in nearly all aspects of education in the last five years alone — new teacher and leader preparation and performance standards, educator evaluation systems, new content standards, new assessments, and more — indicate that educating students continues to be complex work with far-reaching consequences. Meeting those challenges has been the focus of professional learning, which itself has undergone significant changes in that time. As research increasingly reveals what effective professional development is, schools can use what is known about adult learning to better face the challenges of higher standards and to improve student achievement.

In the 1980s, scathing criticism of public education in *A Nation at Risk* caused states to expand their course requirements for graduation and add new and more rigorous curriculum standards to address what was described as "a cafeteria-style curriculum in which the appetizers and desserts can easily be mistaken for the main courses" (National Commission on Excellence in Education, 1983). Education reforms between the late 1980s and the 2000s met with limited success. States determined which courses met the additional course requirements for graduation, and frequently those courses were basic rather than advanced. Schools, particularly high schools, were doing more of the same — more courses, longer school years, and more minutes added to the school day without any significant change in content or pedagogy. Many years later, the policy initiatives from *A*

The introduction of college- and career-ready standards requires new assessments and the data systems to monitor and measure student performance.

Nation at Risk continue to dominate the education landscape, but with only a limited effect on student learning.

Through this period, school systems and states found that achievement gaps existed or even increased based on student background, culture, and socioeconomic status. Researchers identified patterns of course taking as one factor contributing to the achievement gap (Angus & Mirel, 1999; Lucas, 1999).

The move to define common standards for the nation emerged from a number of identified needs, including U.S. students' poor performance on international examinations and a need to strengthen the nation's economy, which depends on a well-educated workforce. A commission of

leading experts led by the National Governors Association and the Council of Chief State School Officers launched the Common Core State Standards initiative to develop a set of national standards in English/language arts and mathematics. Science and social studies standards are expected to follow.

These standards for college- and career-readiness represent a national effort to improve student achievement, reduce variability across classrooms and schools, increase the rigor of student learning outcomes, apply lessons learned from other high-performing countries, and decrease the amount of remediation students need when they enter two- and four-year institutions. The standards set high expectations for all students.

Now, 46 states and several U.S. territories have adopted these standards as the basis for their state curricula. States that have not adopted the standards have established their own college- and career-ready standards. Expected to fully implement the standards in the 2013-14 school year, states and districts have worked to design plans to prepare preservice and inservice teachers to understand the standards and how teaching and learning will change.

Teachers have a complex challenge

Had the introduction and implementation of the Common Core State Standards been the only innovation introduced in 2009, schools and school systems might have been able to focus energy and resources on implementing them. However, the standards have been accompanied by other major initiatives that also require intensive support and resources.

The introduction of college- and career-ready standards requires new assessments and the data systems to monitor and measure student performance. Many states, spurred by the requirements of federal competitive grants, are launching data systems that link educator performance to student academic achievement. Waivers from federal accountability requirements awarded to states are changing how states determine school and student success.

And because student success depends on teacher effectiveness and teacher effectiveness depends on principal effectiveness, approaches for determining educator effectiveness are changing. Decades of ineffective evaluation and professional development systems have provided inadequate feedback and support for educator development throughout their careers. To address these deficiencies, states and districts are introducing new educator effectiveness systems to provide formative and summative evaluations, constructive feedback, and continuous professional development to educators that align more closely with their performance and career stage.

Few changes in education in the last century compare to the breadth and depth of the change ahead for educators, students, parents, and their communities. The work will undoubtedly consume the attention of scholars, researchers, policy and decision makers, and practitioners for decades.

These sweeping reforms require that all educators continuously strive to improve, especially teachers who are responsible for implementing required changes every day in classrooms. To fully and faithfully implement any initiative, teachers need sustained coaching that focuses on the practices aligned with each initiative.

Coaches are a necessary resource

Those who have contributed to developing the standards believe significant changes in content knowledge, instructional practice, and pedagogical content knowledge are essential. In English/ language arts standards, for example, teachers in history, science, and social studies as well as other disciplines will be expected to integrate literacy into their instruction. This will require them to learn about literacy, know how to adapt their instruction to engage students with text, and know how students learn and use literacy within their unique disciplines.

Table 1 summarizes some of the instructional shifts the new standards require. These shifts are

Table 1 Instructional shifts for the Common Core State Standards

ENGLISH LANGUAGE ARTS/LITERACY	MATHEMATICS
Balancing information and literary text	Focus
Building knowledge in the disciplines	Coherence
Staircase of complexity	Fluency
Text-based answers	Deep understanding
Writing from sources	Applications
Academic vocabulary	Dual intensity

Source: http://engageny.org/wp-content/uploads/2012/08/common-core-shifts.pdf.

not just for teachers with primary responsibility for English language arts/literacy and mathematics, but for all teachers.

To make these shifts, districts prepare coaches to support teachers within the following areas:

• Planning instructional units and lessons using new standards, curricula, technologies, and resources.

• Selecting instructional methodologies to teach the knowledge and skills embedded

> Coaches become essential resources in this changing landscape. … They provide personalized, team-based, and schoolwide support to their colleagues.

in the standards.

• Adapting instruction to meet the needs of English language learners and students with special needs.

• Designing rigorous assignments and learning tasks that personalize learning and provide opportunities to apply learning in real-life situations.

• Designing formative assessments and using data from assessments to design instruction.

• Working collaboratively to increase the efficiency and effectiveness of collaborative instructional planning.

• Using data on student performance to reflect on and refine practice.

• Reducing variance across classrooms so that all students have equitable opportunities to learn and succeed.

Because a classroom teacher's daily practice is affected by all of these changes, teachers need substantive support for their ongoing learning as they implement the changes, refine their practices, and reflect on results. This type of support extends well beyond the typical awareness-building professional development that frequently accompanies new initiatives. It involves extensive opportunities to interact with colleagues and with coaches who contribute to deepening teachers' understanding, expanding practice, and refining it to achieve the desired outcomes.

Coaches become essential resources in this changing landscape. In their role as supporters of change, they provide personalized, team-based, and schoolwide support to their colleagues.

Coaches will be responsible for focusing their work on supporting teachers in deepening content knowledge, expanding content-specific pedagogy, and developing a richer understanding of pedagogical content knowledge to produce consistently high results with all students. Coaches also will need to focus on change management support to address personal identity challenges and the frustration, negativity, and resistance that often accompany change of any magnitude.

These are just a few kinds of support coaches will provide teachers as educators make the transition to the new standards. Change research confirms that support over an extended period of time, three to five years or more, is necessary for full implementation. Over this period of time, coaches will move among the roles of learning facilitator, curriculum specialist, instructional specialist, data coach, catalyst for change, and classroom supporter to adapt the support to teachers' particular level of use or stage of concern.

Professional learning enhances coaching

To meet the expectations placed on them for developing others' expertise, coaches, too, need opportunities to develop their own expertise.

Coaches may have limited experience with the content and instructional practice embedded in the Common Core State Standards or other new initiatives introduced since they left their role as a classroom teacher to become a coach. Without their own classroom experience, they may have limited appreciation and perspective for the changes required of teachers within the classroom and know-how for how to bring about those changes. These gaps in coaches' knowledge and experience put coaches at a disadvantage — and the teachers they support at an even bigger one.

Coaches need firsthand experience with planning and implementing instruction related to the new standards in order to develop a deeper level of understanding as well as their own examples to draw from as they interact with teachers. Firsthand experience, even limited to several trials in other teachers' classrooms, provides coaches opportunities to use the new curriculum standards, plan instruction to meet more rigorous learning outcomes, study how students experience a new kind of learning, and understand the cognitive and behavioral shifts necessary to implement college- and career-ready standards. Through reflective practice, especially in dialogue with other coaches or teachers, coaches build an appreciation and empathy for the changes teachers face.

Districts also help coaches prepare for the work by helping them answer the following questions for their interactions with teachers:
- What are college- and career-ready standards?
- What brought about the development and adoption of the Common Core State Standards?
- How do these new standards differ from previous standards?
- What instructional practices are necessary to implement the standards?

- How will assessments of the standards differ?
- What are the core elements of the standards for various grade bands?
- How do the daily and unit curriculum change with these new standards?
- What instructional shifts are necessary for students within various populations, such as English language learners and special education students?
- How will classroom instruction become more personalized to meet the needs of all students?
- How will teachers adapt formative assessments and classwork to align with new standards?
- Given that the Common Core State Standards include literacy across the disciplines, how do teachers in other disciplines incorporate more literacy?
- What do math classrooms look like with less content developed more deeply?

With the implementation of new standards just beginning in many states and districts, these questions are only the tip of the iceberg. They will undoubtedly grow as more becomes known about the changes needed in classrooms, schools, and beyond.

The sweeping changes facing teachers today require a carefully orchestrated plan for implementation that incorporates support for individual teachers, teams of teachers, whole faculties, and teachers across schools. Coaches are a vital part of the change team and an integral part of the future of professional learning. Districts and schools need a deeper knowledge of coaching and its practices in order to prepare for new standards for learning that will increase achievement for all students.

CHAPTER 1

Coaching
matters

School districts across the country have created a laser-like focus on improving student achievement, launching untold numbers and types of initiatives to address needs derived from their student achievement data. They have redirected resources and offered myriad professional learning opportunities for teachers to improve their instructional practices and to differentiate their instruction to meet the needs of a wide range of learners in their classrooms. All of these efforts and approaches are focused on positively impacting student achievement.

While some teachers return to their classrooms after professional development and make earnest attempts to use the information they learned, they frequently have little or no follow-up at their schools, or the follow-up that occurs is provided from the central office level. More often than not, teachers have a low level of implementation of current initiatives or are unclear about what a high level of implementation looks like. As a result, even specially funded programs and new initiatives such as Title 1, STEM, and other intervention programs in many of the nation's schools and districts are failing to impact student achievement to a high degree.

Other schools and districts have learned that professional learning is a powerful intervention for increasing teaching effectiveness and student learning if it incorporates classroom- and school-focused support in the form of coaching, that gives educators on-site and sometimes online support to integrate new curricula or pedagogies into their practice effectively and efficiently. Coaches, as members of the school leadership team, align teachers' professional learning with school goals and facilitate the professional learning that occurs at the school.

Coaching influences teacher practice, and some studies have found that coaching also affects student achievement and school culture.

A coach personalizes teachers' learning by understanding each teacher's current state of practice and the conditions in which that teacher practices, and by having deep knowledge of the practices being implemented. With expertise in content, pedagogy, and coaching, a coach is able to support teachers in making desired changes in their knowledge, skills, practices, and dispositions and is able to contribute to creating a culture of collaboration and peer support.

Jane Creasy and Fred Paterson identify the key benefits of coaching as "improving a whole school or department, personalizing professional learning for staff, promoting self-directed professional learning, creating a learning-centered mode of professional

dialogue, and building capacity for leadership" (2005, p. 20). Mary Jean Taylor (2008) notes that principals see additional benefits of coaching: "They reported seeing more conversations about instruction, more use of student data for instructional decisions, greater implementation of ideas and strategies presented in professional development, new teachers getting up to speed faster, and veteran teachers 'modernizing' their instructional strategies. They felt their decision making improved as a result of the coaches' instructional expertise and depth of knowledge about teaching throughout the school. They felt better able to actually implement their school improvement strategies, more informed and connected to the district pool of professional development expertise, and more effective in guiding their staff" (p. 4).

Coaching alters many aspects of schools. Most notably, coaching influences teacher practice, and some studies have found that coaching also affects student achievement and school culture. (See sidebar pp. 10-12.)

Most who have participated in effective coaching programs — whether they are teachers, coaches, or principals — immediately are able to identify coaching's benefits. Yet research over the last two decades is disparate and insufficient.

Some studies suggest that coaching makes little difference in increasing student achievement and improving teacher practice (Garet et al., 2008, 2010, 2011). Other studies provide a different view.

What is evident across the various studies is that the practice of coaching varies substantially from situation to situation. The variations affect the work of coaches and the results of coaching. Whether coaching works, at this stage of the research, seems to depend on how coaching is implemented, the longevity of coaching practices, the support provided by principals, the culture of the school, and the preparation of coaches (Borman, Feger &

Kawakami, 2006). Done well, coaching works to change teacher practice and student achievement. Done inconsistently and inadequately, coaching seems to have little or no effect. The conditions in which coaching occurs matter as much as the design of the intervention.

Nations that outperform the United States on international assessments invest heavily in professional learning and build time within the workday for ongoing, sustained teacher development and collaboration.

The United States is far behind in providing public school teachers with opportunities to participate in extended learning opportunities and productive collaborative communities. Effective professional development:

- Is intensive, ongoing, and connected to practice;
- Focuses on the teaching and learning of specific academic content;
- Is connected to other school initiatives; and
- Builds strong working relationships among teachers.

Coaching supports teachers in examining their practice through intensive, ongoing professional learning. Coaching must be embedded into teachers' daily lives, however, and considered part of their everyday work, not something extra or voluntary. This will require significant changes in how the school day is shaped so teachers can engage in learning, even while teaching students, and have adequate time to collaborate.

Coaching can produce results

Coaching as a school improvement intervention has tremendous potential but requires significant support to deliver on its promise. Although not all coaching programs are effective, most coaches influence teaching, student learning, and school culture. Simply identifying a willing candidate and calling him or her coach, however, won't lead to success.

Success comes from developing the coach's expertise, providing ongoing support and supervision, and rigorously monitoring and evaluating coaches' work and effects. When coaching programs are less effective, many will question the benefits of coaching.

Quality coaching is an expensive intervention. As school boards and school system leaders make

> The conditions in which coaching occurs matter as much as the design of the intervention.

difficult budgetary decisions, they certainly will question the investment in coaching even while human capital constitutes the greatest percentage of school system budgets — often 80% or more. However, school systems that have in place clearly articulated coaching programs are rarely disappointed in the results. Coaches' work contributes to better teaching, improved student learning, and a culture of continuous improvement.

Creating a sound infrastructure, practices, parameters, and relationships significantly increases the likelihood that coaching will work. To realize the full potential of coaching as a professional learning model that will produce results for teachers and students, district and school leaders must invest in creating the environment, structures, and conditions for coaches and coaching to succeed.

Coaches are vital to school and instructional improvement. They are the intermediaries between administrators who expect high-level student results and the teachers who must bring about those results.

Coaching can result in increased student achievement, changed teacher practice, and improved school culture if school and district leaders, coaches, and teachers attend to the conditions for success.

Coaching matters.

Coaching research and evaluations
Research and evaluations point out what is known about effective coaching.

Coaching affects teacher practice.

- A 1984 study of 80 schools with peer coaching found that "(d)escription, modeling, practice, and feedback resulted in a 16% to 19% transfer of skill to classroom use. … However, when coaching was added to the staff development, approximately 95% of the teachers implemented the new skills in their classrooms" (Bush, 1984, p. 197).

- William T. Truesdale (2003) found that after 15 weeks, teachers who did not receive coaching stopped using the new learning, while those who received coaching increased the transfer of the training to their classrooms.

- In a review (2010) of the instructional coaching program in Jeffco (Jefferson County, Colo.) Public Schools, Cindy Harrison, Heather Clifton, and Chris Bryan found that the majority of teachers and principals who participated in the study reported that instructional coaching affected teacher practice.

- Jim Knight (2007) found a 70% increase in instructional practices modeled by coaches. Similar results occur in other studies Knight conducted (2004, 2006).

- Bruce Joyce and Beverly Showers (1995) reported that the likelihood of transferring new learning from professional development into practice increases nearly 80% when coaching is added to an explanation of theory, demonstration, and low-risk practice.

- Showers (1982, 1984) states that teachers who receive coaching are more likely to incorporate new teaching practices into their classrooms than teachers who are not coached. In addition, students of teachers who were coached showed significantly higher gains in achievement test scores than did students whose teachers had not been coached.

Coaching can have an effect on student achievement.

- A 2006 study by The Learning Network reported steady growth in student achievement over five years in 4th-grade student reading scores when teacher leaders worked as literacy coaches in their schools: from 29% achieving proficiency in 1999 to 86% proficient on state standardized exams in 2004. (However, the research design makes it difficult to determine whether the teacher leader coaches were responsible for improved student performance.)

- A study of math and science coaching in South Carolina schools showed substantial increases in student achievement on state assessments (South Carolina's Coalition for Math & Science, 2008).

- A randomized control study examined the effects of a coaching program for secondary teachers on improving teacher-student interactions to address student motivation, effort, and achievement. The study found that students of teachers who received coaching "had a significant net gain relative to the control group … (that) equates to an average increase in student achievement from the 50th to the 59th percentile" (Allen et al., 2011, p. 1035).

- Gina Biancarosa, Anthony Bryk, and Emily Dexter's 2010 study of instructional coaching found that coaching contributed to a 32% increase in student learning gains after the third year. The study tracked student achievement from one year before coaching began through the third year of implementation.
- Underperforming students in Texas increased their achievement significantly when their teachers experienced coaching (Redell, 2004).
- South Carolina students in a statewide math and science initiative showed a 27% increase in the number scoring proficient and advanced in a single school year in one elementary school where teachers received coaching and no other changes were made (Dempsey, 2007).

Coaching's effect may take time.

- A series of studies of reading and math intervention programs using professional development that included traditional workshops, coaching, and collaborative teacher work found no statistically significant effects of the intervention on student achievement or changes in teacher practice. The studies examined the effects of the professional development intervention over two years (Garet et al., 2011).
- A comprehensive study of the effects of Florida's middle school literacy program, which included coaching, reports that while peers and principals view coaches as having a positive effect on their schools, they had little effect on student achievement (Marsh et al., 2008). The program studied provided important information on what matters in coaching, however. For example, the length of time a school had a coach had a statistically significant effect on student achievement. This finding suggests that coaching's effects are greater over time. District and state leaders have used this study to strengthen the features of their coaching programs.
- Patricia Campbell and Nathaniel Malkus concluded at the end of a three-year study that students who were in schools with an elementary mathematics coach had significantly higher scores on their state's mathematics achievement tests (grades 3 through 5) than did students in the control schools without coaches (2011). "This effect only emerged as knowledgeable specialists gained experience and as schools' instructional and administrative staffs learned and worked together," they write. "Simply allocating funds and then filling the position of an elementary mathematics specialist in a school will not yield increased student achievement. The specialists in this study influenced the beliefs about mathematics teaching and learning held by the teachers with whom they were highly engaged" (Campbell & Malkus, 2010, pp. 25-26).

The way coaching occurs matters.

- A study in Los Angeles found that direct coach-teacher interactions were more likely to lead to changes in teacher practice than small group interactions. "Coaching that was ongoing and directly related to classroom instruction," the research team reports, "provided greater evidence of potential and actual improvement than did irregular interactions or activities directed at larger group meetings" (Rivera, Burley, & Sass, 2004, p. 5).

- A study of instructional coaching in high schools from 2005-10 concluded that the frequency of principal and coach meetings was related to student achievement. The district demonstrating the most significant growth in student achievement had almost daily interaction between the coach and principal (Sumner, 2011, p. 8).

- Coaching improved teacher practice in the Washoe County (Nev.) School District, an evaluation found. A triangulation study verified a relationship among: the frequency of coaching, the program's duration, and coach experience and student achievement. In addition, the evaluation concluded, "The district plays an important role in shaping and supporting ICoach program effectiveness by: 1) articulating clear expectations related to student achievement and helping schools and coaches focus coaching on achieving those expectations, and 2) providing ongoing support for the selection, professional development, and evaluation of coaching" (Taylor, 2008, p. 4).

- Another study (Biancarosa, Bryk, Atteberry, & Hough, 2010) found a difference in schools based on the number of coaching sessions teachers received. "In the 'high-coaching' school, although value-added scores started out below average, they increased during the study," the authors write. "In the 'low-coaching' school, school-level value-added scores were above average but subsequently declined. … The 'high-coaching' school also saw … teaching (become) more equitably effective for students, while in the 'low-coaching' school, variation among teachers increased so that teaching effectiveness became more inequitably distributed" (p. 3).

- Allison Atteberry and Anthony Bryk (2011) report that school factors influenced teacher engagement in coaching. They found that teachers who acknowledged a strong sense of responsibility toward fellow teachers and were more committed to their school participated in more coaching regardless of the school's size. Principal support of professional development also correlated with more coaching.

- Liz Browne evaluated a subject-specific peer coaching program in the United Kingdom and concluded: "The peer coaching approach has been shown to encourage professional dialogue and practitioner confidence. This in turn has impacted on learner knowledge and skills leading to innovative and exciting practice" (2006, p. 42).

- An evaluation of the Pennsylvania High School Coaching Initiative showed that coaching influences teacher practice and student achievement. Coaches build a sense of community and a culture of improvement that produce schoolwide improvement and student achievement (Brown et al., 2007). The evaluators note that coaching works through the phases of teacher growth and change before it affects student achievement.

- In a study comparing six schools in the Fairfax (Va.) County Public Schools district with high implementation of coaching and five schools rated as low implementers, high-implementing schools demonstrated significantly higher pass rates on Virginia's math benchmarks than the low-implementing schools, even though the schools had no significant differences in baseline rates. These findings suggest that instructional coaches had a positive effect on school culture and academics, and that their level of impact varied with the way coaches were used (Fairfax County Public Schools, 2008).

Creating a
coaching program

All new initiatives begin similarly, with identifying the gap between what exists and a desired state, identifying the root cause of that gap, and then researching solutions to the identified problem. Involving a leadership team of representative stakeholders can help, even in the earliest stages, to improve the chance for a program to succeed. The team's work may change over time and new members may be added, but representation is critical.

When the gap is in student performance and the problem is teaching effectiveness, one viable and evidence-based intervention is coaching. Coaching enhances professional learning and the implementation of effective practices. Although the process outlined here can be used to develop other intervention programs a team may choose for its context, the focus and examples here are on coaching.

Developing a program begins with developing goals. The goal emerges when the team analyzes the current state and identifies the root cause. Many coaching programs are designed with a single goal in place:

Improve student achievement by improving teaching effectiveness.

or

Increase student achievement on state assessments in literacy and math by 30% in grades 2-12 by 2014.

Developing a goal is the first step of the process of designing and implementing an effective coaching program.

A coaching program's goal or measure of success is best stated in terms of student success. Keeping student achievement as the program's focus reaps benefits later in the program development and implementation process. Coaching's primary goal is to improve student learning. Coaches mediate teachers' practice by supporting teachers in improving their practice so they are able to teach all students more effectively. Without continually holding student success as the primary focus of coaching, coaches and teachers miss their primary means of knowing whether coaching matters. Developing a goal is the first step of the process of designing and implementing an effective coaching program. The leadership team will research coaching's effectiveness, gather information about successful coaching models, and learn about different approaches to coaching. Building team members' foundational knowledge will help them make a decision informed less by personal opinion and more by verifiable, reliable information.

Another way to build the team's foundational understanding is to visit schools or districts that have coaching. If the leadership team prepares questions and gathers standard information, these visits are opportunities to observe coaching in practice and develop a greater understanding of what conditions lead to a successful program. Talking with school principals, teachers, and coaches can help team members understand the complexities of coaching. Team members can collect artifacts used in the program — coaches' job descriptions, sample partnership agreements between the coach and teachers or between the coach and principal, goal-setting templates for teachers, templates for data conversations, or sample agendas for introducing the program to the staff, and so on — to help later in planning and designing their own program and creating their own tools.

Conducting focus groups with stakeholder representatives — including principals, teachers, resource staff, and others — can lead to broad-based ownership of the ensuing design and implementation. Get input from practicing professionals about their understanding of the identified problem, their interest in meeting the defined goal, and their perceptions about the potential impact of coaching. Conversations with stakeholders also shed light on people's fears and any potential barriers to success — information that program developers can use in their planning.

Plan the program

When district and/or school leaders are deliberate and thoughtful about beginning a coaching program, they are more likely to succeed. The overall planning and development process can take from a few months to 18 months or more. The following steps can guide the planning process.

Sample focus group questions

- What factors within the school's control most affect student learning?

- What is the role of instruction in student learning?

- What challenges do teachers today face in instruction?

- What challenges do teachers face in helping all students achieve high results?

- What supports are most likely to improve teaching effectiveness?

- What might motivate teachers to participate in coaching?

- What are the barriers to teachers participating in coaching?

- What effect has peer support had on your instruction? On student achievement in your classroom?

- What are some possible benefits of coaching?

- What are some possible pitfalls of coaching?

Form a steering committee/ leadership team

Convene a representative steering committee that includes teachers, resource staff, principals, and central office personnel. Include a teacher representative of the teachers association to be certain that teachers' voices are included in the decision-making process.

Create a charge statement

Write a clear charge statement outlining the general outcomes and identify questions the steering committee might address, along with a reasonable timeline for program design. An example of the overall charge to the steering committee might be: To provide a support structure for teacher success with upcoming expectations, that is Common Core State Standards, teacher evaluation, and so on, through the creation of a powerful instructional coaching model that positively impacts student achievement.

Write a clear charge statement outlining the general outcomes.

Clearly defining parameters of the steering committee's work may help the committee to avoid pitfalls in the decision-making process. Examples of parameters are:

- The steering committee will make final recommendations to the assistant superintendent for learning services.

- The superintendent's cabinet will make final decisions about the program.

- The committee will work within current budget allocations for full-time equivalents.

Steering committee program design questions

- What are the desired outcomes for the coaching program? What outcomes are expected after the first year? After the third?

- What main roles will coaches take? Should these roles change over time? If so, how?

- What is the coach's job description?

- Who will coach? What is the hiring process?

- What characteristics of coaches are likely to make a difference in student achievement?

- What coaching behaviors are expected or appropriate?

- How will we ensure that coaches remain connected to classroom practice?

- How will we evaluate the coaching program?

- How will we define confidentiality as it pertains to the coaches' work?

- Who will train coaches? How often?

- Who will be coached?

- How will conflicts that arise between coaches and teachers or administrators be addressed?

- Who will supervise and evaluate the coaches?

- How will coaches receive feedback on the impact of their work?

- How will coaches communicate with others about their work?

- What is the relationship between coaches and new teacher mentors, instructional coordinators, reading specialists?

- What will be the same about the program design at all levels? What will be different for elementary, middle, and high schools?

Table 2.1 Sample timeline for the coaching steering committee

DATES	TASKS
July 1 to December 1	Coaching steering committee designs the program, shares a draft for feedback, modifies the design based on the feedback, and presents the plan to the decision-making authorities.
January	Decisions are made about the program.
February	Roll out the program.
March	Begin the hiring process.
April 15	Hire coaches.
May 15	Complete coach placements.
June through August	Provide professional development for coaches, principals, and teachers.

Define a timeline

Define a timeline for the work to help maintain focus and ensure productivity. A sample time-line for the coaching steering committee can be seen in Table 2.1.

Define outcomes

Defining the desired outcomes of the coaching program — and ways to measure the outcomes — may be the steering committee's most important work. Chapter 11 on evaluating coaching and coaches has examples of how coaching's outcomes align with school and district improvement goals.

When coaching seeks to achieve the school or district goals, coaching is integrally linked to core work. When coaching's outcomes differ from the school's or district's core goals, coaching may be viewed as an add-on and eventually considered unnecessary. Sample district outcomes, adapted from Naperville Community School District #203, are:

Year 1

- Increased job-embedded and collaborative professional learning opportunities for individual teachers and building-based communities of learning.
- Increased capacity of teachers to meet the needs of *all* students and implement the teaching and learning framework, expected performance standards, and core instructional practices.
- Increased facilitation of teacher collaborative planning and reflection that increases the school's culture of collaboration.
- Increased implementation of the four coaching roles — classroom supporter (partner), instructional specialist, data coach, and learning facilitator — and building- and district-level support for the coaching role.

Year 2
- Increased student performance on state and district measures with an emphasis on closing achievement gaps.
- Increased instructional and curricular support to implement Common Core State Standards and educational changes associated with Common Core implementation.
- Increased integration of literacy in all disciplines.

- Increased integration of mathematics across the disciplines.
- Increased instructional capacity of teachers to meet the needs of students and to implement the teaching and learning framework, expected performance standards, and core instructional practices.

Year 3
- Increased student performance on state and district measures with an emphasis on closing achievement gaps.

Types of coaching

Joellen Killion and Cindy Harrison (2006) describe different types of coaching, each with a distinct focus or purpose. The types share many commonalities as well. In fact, distinguishing the various forms of coaching in practice may be difficult because many use similar processes. Types of coaching reported in the literature include:

- **Challenge coaching:** Coaches support individuals or teams of teachers in addressing persistent problems in their instruction.

- **Cognitive Coaching**[SM]**:** Coaches engage in conversations with teachers about planning, reflecting, and problem solving with the intent of building autonomy and interdependence.

- **Collegial coaching:** Coaches work as peers with individuals or teacher teams to strengthen their collegiality, collaborative skills, and instructional practice.

- **Content-focused coaching:** Coaches focus their interactions with teachers on content-specific instruction, planning and assessment curriculum, content knowledge, and pedagogical content knowledge.

- **Instructional coaching:** Coaches interact with teachers on all aspects of instruction, including planning, assessing learning, and differentiating to meet learners' needs.

- **Mentoring:** Coaches focus on supporting novice teachers to build their instructional expertise and support their acclimation to their school.

- **Peer coaching:** Teachers provide coaching support to one another, typically focused on a new area of learning, in a collegial, nonevaluative relationship to advance their individual expertise with the learning.

- Increased teacher leadership in instructional planning, effective practices in instruction, data-informed culture, and collaborative culture.
- Increased level of implementation of co-teaching, co-planning, planning and data analysis structures, and building-based professional learning.
- Increase in purposeful use of collaborative planning time.

Define the coaches' roles

Decide what roles coaches will take during years one, two, and three. Limiting the number of roles can help ensure coaches gain a higher level of expertise and greater success.

Once roles are selected, specify exactly what each role will entail in your district so that everyone is clear about what a coach does and does not do. Creating an is/is not list can be helpful (see Chapter 5 on the roles of coaches and supporting tools).

- **Peer consultation:** Peers commit to work together for their mutual benefit and provide supportive feedback in a collegial, nonsupervisory relationship in which individuals may accept or reject feedback.

- **Technical coaching:** Coaches work with teachers to support the implementation of specific, newly acquired instructional practices into routine classroom practice.

Many coaches use multiple types of coaching in their work. They may move seamlessly from technical to peer to relationship coaching as needed to support their clients.

In some coaching programs, the specific assumptions underlying coaching's goals, design, and operations are more strongly aligned with a particular approach. For example, a district with an explicit instructional framework or that is implementing a new program may focus on developing faithful implementation.

Some coaching types are built on a distinct theory, while others are less distinctive and share features. In a literature review specifically of instructional coaching, Jennifer Borman, Stephanie Feger, and Nobuaki Kawakami explore the underlying theories guiding the design of many coaching programs.

"Across programs described in the literature, instructional coaching may fall at differing points along differing continua," they write (2006, p. 4). "The degree to which coaching is consultative or directive, collaborative or supervisory, focused on inquiry or teacher behavior, peer-to-peer or expert-to-novice has significant ramifications for research and practice. Again, these are not pure dichotomies, but differences in degree and kind. Some of the accounts in the literature explicitly situate instructional coaching within a given theory of learning or change, but many do not."

Gather feedback

Solicit feedback on the plan from stakeholders and constituents who will be affected by coaching. Plan how to seek feedback from constituents to ensure the message is communicated uniformly and questions are answered accurately and in a timely way. Some districts develop specific talking points or question-and-answer documents that succinctly describe the proposal. This sharing is an opportunity to genuinely seek feedback rather than to sell the program. Eager program developers may find it difficult to listen to feedback because they are invested in the elements of their

Having a clear definition of coaching's essential elements will contribute to the program's integrity and help determine to what extent any variations in implementation affect student and teacher learning.

design. Each time the proposed plan is shared, collect feedback and bring it to the steering committee for consideration. Make ongoing revisions to the plan based on the feedback and any new research, taking into account modifications the committee perceives to be aligned with the desired outcomes for the program.

Roll out a plan

The initial rollout of the coaching initiative may be launched at the same time the hiring process is designed or before. It is important to ensure all constituents receive the same message and questions are answered in a way that instills confidence in the stakeholders that the design is well developed.

In addition, the steering committee may make judicious use of time by rolling out the plan at all sites at the beginning of a school year or at the end of the year before implementation. While schools may have differences that result in small variations in how the program is implemented, having a clear definition of coaching's essential elements will contribute to the program's integrity and help determine to what extent any variations in implementation affect student and teacher learning.

Create a hiring plan

Create a plan for hiring and placing coaches. The steering committee may ask a human resources group to design a hiring plan and to provide input into the process, or human resources representatives may join the steering committee to complete this work.

Writing a job description aligned with program outcomes is integral to the process. Clearly describing the link between district goals and the coaching program's desired outcomes enables planners to specify coaches' specific roles and duties. Decide what roles and duties are required of all coaches and which ones schools may adapt based on their own context. As the focus of coaches' work shifts over time based on student and teacher learning needs, schools will need ongoing communication about the coaches' roles. Next, consider and decide who will screen and interview candidates. Chapter 6 on hiring and placing coaches describes this step in greater detail.

Provide professional learning for coaches

Professional learning about the specific requirements of coaching will contribute to the program's success. Allocate time for professional learning before coaches begin work to help them gain confidence in the role. Time the professional learning so that coaches can talk with their supervisors and make some initial partnership agreements to help ensure the program gets off to a good start at the school.

Coaches also need continuous support throughout the year, ideally a full or half day a week. One day per month of professional learning support is a minimum. Especially when coaches are new to the position and the program is new, the coaches need opportunities to share their work with each other, learn from each other, and collectively solve problems in order to build a strong network with each other in and outside of meetings. As coaches become more proficient in coaching skills, professional learning may take different forms, such as coaches meeting in communities of practice.

Incorporate a gradual release model and differentiate the professional learning to ensure various learning needs are addressed. Consider using webinars, face-to-face meetings, learning walks, learning laboratories, and other designs. Chapter 7 will help in designing professional learning for coaches.

Evaluate the program

Follow the steps in Chapter 11 to design an evaluation. Additional resources include:

- *Assessing Impact: Evaluating Staff Development*, by Joellen Killion. Corwin Press, 2008.
- Innovation Configuration maps from *Taking the Lead: New Roles for Teachers and School-Based Coaches*, by Joellen Killion and Cindy Harrison. National Staff Development Council, 2006.

- Innovation Configuration maps from *Standards for Professional Learning*. Learning Forward, 2011.

Other evaluation tools might include implementation checklists that measure the level of implementation of a particular curriculum content area program to compare with student achievement in that content, or a checklist to assess teachers' level of use of the coach and coaching resources.

> Coaches need opportunities to share their work with each other, learn from each other, and collectively solve problems in order to build a strong network with each other in and outside of meetings.

Monitor the program

Define and communicate how the program will be monitored on an ongoing basis. Annual evaluations provide important information for improving the program. Attention to tensions, challenges, successes, and trouble spots that emerge during implementation is important so issues can be addressed quickly to increase the program's potential for success.

If the steering committee has not remained as the oversight team, the district might appoint a new team to oversee the program. Whether the same team stays on in this new role or a new one is appointed, the team's work should be grounded in data and evidence. Systems, such as communication and feedback loops that allow information to flow freely between the oversight team and program participants, should be in place that make the work expedient and transparent.

Scenario

The suburban district of 15,000 students had had school-based literacy coordinators for eight years. The program was popular with teachers but had done little to change reading achievement, especially for English language learners and special needs students. The literacy coordinators' work varied from school to school, and two-thirds of their time was spent on managerial tasks such as coordinating tests and providing teachers with curricular resources.

When the state adopted Common Core State Standards, the district planned that K-2 teachers would implement the standards immediately, followed in a year by all other grade-level teachers. District leaders recognized, however, that teachers would need additional support to change their instruction.

While area districts had implemented coaching programs, this district had not considered the option because of declining resources. Now repurposing the literacy coordinators to create a coaching program made sense.

District leaders knew they needed to carefully design the coaching program. Adopting a neighboring district's program would be easier, but their previous experiences with the literacy coordinator program showed them they needed to be more structured and more specific about the coaching program's design in order to increase student achievement, especially because coaching was intended to support implementation of the Common Core State Standards.

Tia Hernandez, the assistant superintendent of teaching and learning, knew she would need central office, building principal, and teacher support to create a successful program. She began by researching professional learning designs, using coaching as the main model. She visited districts with successful coaching programs and contacted an expert to help her sort through her thinking. She and others in her department spent months discussing instructional coaching models and what might be effective in their district.

Hernandez decided to start with a steering committee facilitated by the field expert. She recruited her best thinkers for the steering committee and made sure all stakeholder groups were represented, including the president of the teachers association. The committee met for three months, studying model programs to determine core features, setting the program's goals, and addressing a teachers association concern about hiring coaches because the literacy coordinators would be affected. The committee proposed opening all coaching positions and guaranteeing the current literacy coordinators an interview.

Committee members carefully planned the announcement to staff. They met first with principals and literacy coordinators to share the proposed changes and get input. The teachers association executive committee also weighed in on the proposal.

Once the committee had met with these groups, spokespeople met with the superintendent's cabinet to provide the feedback they had collected and final recommendations. The cabinet accepted the plan, making minor changes for budgeting reasons. Next, the superintendent presented the plan to the school board, which endorsed it and encouraged the superintendent to move ahead with a rigorous program evaluation over three years.

The committee formed a subgroup to discuss evaluation parameters and prepared to gather baseline data in all the schools in which coaches would be placed. By early May, coaches had been hired for each school, baseline data had been gathered, and principals and staff prepared to transition to the new coaching program. Before school ended for the year, coaches even had opportunities to meet with teaching staffs to discuss summer professional learning plans. The new coaches, more than half of whom were former literacy coordinators, prepared for intensive summer professional learning focused on coaching skills and the Common Core State Standards. The transition had gone smoothly.

Reflection questions

- What are the advantages of detailed planning for a new coaching program or redesigning an existing one? What consequences might the program and district face without such planning?

- What recommendations in this chapter might apply to a review of an existing coaching program to strengthen its overall effectiveness and results for teachers and students?

- Within the context of your school community, whom would you want to participate in focus groups and on a steering committee? What are your reasons for wanting to engage these individuals?

- Considering Hernandez's actions in the scenario to revamp her district's coaching program, which strategies make sense to you and what advice would you give her based on your own experience?

- What information from this chapter will be useful in your next review of an existing program to continue to improve its effectiveness and results? Which components of your program are in place and working, and which are missing and need attention?

Recommendations for

Central office administrators

- Include representatives of all stakeholder groups on a steering committee.
- Seek steering committee members who will stay together for at least one year to serve as an oversight committee once the program begins.
- Research effective coaching programs and models prior to or in the early stages of program development.
- Link the coaching program with school district and school priorities and goals.
- Review district policies and contracts to be certain the proposed program aligns with existing programs, or identify changes needed.
- Prepare clear written descriptions of the proposed program to discuss with stakeholder groups.
- Respond to stakeholders' input by adapting the proposed program.
- Develop written descriptions of the approved program explaining stakeholder groups' roles and responsibilities.

Building administrators

- Provide the steering committee with honest feedback as it develops the program.
- Communicate clearly and positively to staff about the proposed program.
- Share staff feedback about the proposed program with the steering committee.
- Communicate clearly and positively to staff about the program once it is approved.
- Provide continual feedback to the steering committee to make ongoing improvements to the program.
- Communicate challenges, problems, or questions to the steering committee.
- Provide constructive feedback to the coach(es) about implementation of the coaching program in the school.

Coaches

- Communicate clearly to staff about the program.
- Implement the program with fidelity.
- Seek input from colleagues and the principal about the coaching program.
- Share the input with the district steering committee accurately and objectively.
- Engage in problem solving and seek support for any challenges.
- Collect accurate data for the program evaluation.
- Monitor how your time is spent, and adjust how time is allocated based on expectations for defined roles.

TOOL INDEX
Chapter 2

	TOOL	PURPOSE
2.1	**Framework for successful coaching programs**	Use this tool as a checklist of the components of effective coaching programs.
2.2	**Instructional coaching model charge statement**	Guide the steering committee's work with this example of a charge statement.
2.3	**Sample timeline for designing a coaching program**	Base your timing for creating and rolling out a new coaching program on this example.
2.4	**Sample coaching committee agenda**	Review this example of a steering committee meeting agenda.
2.5	**Roles of the learning support coach**	Understand the specificity needed to delineate coaching roles.

To download tools, see www.learningforward.org/publications/coachingmatters

Characteristics
of effective coaches

Just as the quality of teaching determines student success, the quality of coaching determines how well coaching succeeds with teachers. And just as the quality of teaching depends on the teacher's expertise and classroom conditions, coaching depends on two factors: the coach's skills and the conditions in which coaching occurs.

Joellen Killion and Cindy Harrison (2006) say that effective school-based coaches share core beliefs that influence their approach to working with others, as well as having teaching expertise, coaching skills, relationship skills, content expertise, and leadership skills. Table 3.1 elaborates on these characteristics. Coaches, mentors, and teacher leaders with these characteristics, in the right conditions, can have a significant effect on teachers' instruction and student learning.

Table 3.1 Characteristics of effective school-based coaches

Beliefs	Teaching expertise	Coaching skills
An effective coach: • Is willing to learn. • Has a passion for ongoing development. • Believes in others' capacity to grow and develop. • Has the attitude that everyone is important. • Does not presume to have "The Answer." • Understands his or her own assumptions and makes those transparent. • Is committed to continuous improvement. • Has moral purpose. • Can let go of feeling responsible for another person's behaviors.	An effective coach: • Is skilled in instructional planning. • Demonstrates success in his or her work as a classroom teacher. • Reflects on his or her own practice. • Articulates his or her own practice. • Uses multiple methods of assessing students. • Has strong classroom organization and management. • Is fluent in multiple methods of delivering instruction.	An effective coach: • Understands and applies knowledge about adult development. • Diagnoses teachers' needs. • Aligns support to teachers' identified needs. • Communicates effectively. • Listens skillfully. • Uses effective questioning skills. • Understands and employs a specific reflection process.
Relationship skills	**Content expertise**	**Leadership skills**
An effective coach: • Has good interpersonal relationships. • Wants to be part of a team. • Fosters trust. • Works effectively with teachers and principals. • Is respected by peers. • Has patience for the learning process.	An effective coach: • Possesses and applies appropriate, in-depth content knowledge. • Uses research and theory to support instructional decisions. • Establishes a collegial learning environment to support teachers in reflecting on their practice. • Stays current with changes in curricula and new instructional practices.	An effective coach: • Stays abreast of best practices in professional learning. • Engages others in developing plans for improvement. • Maintains a productive culture. • Communicates the school's vision. • Aligns work with school goals. • Uses data to make decisions. • Understands and applies knowledge about change.

Source: Killion, J. & Harrison, C. (2006). *Taking the lead: New roles for coaches and teacher leaders*. Oxford, OH: National Staff Development Council.

Beliefs

The coach's beliefs, attitudes, values, and dispositions are the basis for being able to work effectively with teachers. Fundamental dispositions include a willingness to learn and a passion for ongoing development — beliefs that the coach must convey to others. Effective coaches recognize that coaches, as well as the teachers they serve, must continually seek deeper understanding. Conveying a positive attitude about lifelong learning helps coaches model continuous learning for teachers.

Effective coaches convey the belief that others are capable of and committed to learning, growing, and developing as professional educators. Coaches who are tempted to assume that teachers who resist being coached are either unable or unwilling to learn first examine their own core beliefs.

Just as the classroom teacher is expected to believe that every child can learn and discover how to motivate and work with all learners, effective coaches believe that every teacher can learn, and they work to find ways to influence and engage teachers as learners. Committing to continuous improvement and the attitude that everyone in the learning community is important leads to a climate of respect, collegiality, and collective responsibility.

Effective coaches, regardless of their years in the classroom or as coaches, strive to understand each teacher's needs, strengths, and goals, and they readily admit that they do not have a solution for all teachers' problems. They do not assume they have The Answer that a teacher needs. They think aloud with teachers, transparently revealing and making public the data on which they base their assumptions and the thinking processes they used to arrive at their decisions.

Effective coaches demonstrate their beliefs by working side by side with teachers and teaching teams to support them in continuous learning to strengthen the quality of teaching. Coaches also model the belief that all students can succeed by using data; by designing, implementing, and evaluating classroom interventions; by using formative assessments; and by examining student work.

Effective coaches release themselves from taking responsibility for others' behaviors. According to Mary Jane Even, "Adult learning is voluntary in all its dimensions — participation, acquisition, and outcomes" (1987, p. 22). Adults generally do not learn in an authentic way without opportunities to choose some, if not all, aspects of the learning (Knight, 2007).

If an adult learner chooses not to learn or grow, an insightful coach does not blame the individual, dismiss the opportunity, or abdicate responsibility. Instead, the coach looks for opportunities to influence the teacher in other ways, no matter how small or insignificant the opportunity may seem. The coach does not reproach himself

> Effective coaches convey the belief that others are capable of and committed to learning, growing, and developing as professional educators.

for not having the power to change a less willing teacher or exert force to engender engagement. Rather, a coach acknowledges that providing different opportunities for learning may be necessary to bring along those less willing, and, ultimately, to accept that not everyone chooses change willingly. There clearly are times when supervisory efforts are needed to initiate change.

Teaching expertise

A prerequisite for becoming a coach often is having demonstrated expertise as a classroom teacher. Teachers who view coaches as successful teachers are more open to coaching. Researchers studying literacy coaches in Florida reported:

> In one school, teachers argued that their coach had credibility because she "did our job" and had many years of experience with and knowledge about teaching reading to diverse learners. As a result, one teacher explained, "I know it's going to work if she suggests it." Similarly, teachers in another school were quick to point out the vast knowledge base

Having teaching expertise adds to

coaches' credibility.

of their coach. "She's the most effective reading coach I've worked with. She definitely knows her stuff," said one teacher. In contrast, a perceived lack of teaching experience and knowledge in another case study school accounted for some teachers' less enthusiastic appraisal of their reading coach. One social studies teacher stated, "I don't think she had the reading background. … If you were to be a reading coach, you'd have taught reading for years so if someone came to you, you could say 'Oh, you know what, I tried this one time.' So there is more of a background knowledge to help." As a result, many teachers in this school reported approaching experienced teachers, not the coach, for help with instructional matters. (Marsh et al., 2008, pp. 63-64)

Having teaching expertise adds to coaches' credibility and is the foundation for supporting teachers' work. Coaches' classroom teaching experience makes it possible for them to demonstrate lessons, co-teach, co-plan, or give teachers constructive feedback. Coaches have more credibility when they are fluent in multiple instructional methods that meet the needs of a range of learners,

have covered several curricular areas, and know the theoretical or research base for making decisions about instruction.

Effective coaches also are able to reflect on their practices and articulate how they make decisions about implementing the practices they choose, modeling these skills for teachers as they help teachers to achieve the same level. They are able to help teachers decide which assessments to use to measure student progress. They effectively use formative and summative assessments to help teachers prepare students for district benchmark and summative assessments, and they help teams of teachers develop common assessments or individual teachers develop classroom assessments. Coaches also use their expertise in assessment to gather data and plan strategies to meet teachers' needs.

Finally, coaches who have deep knowledge about and strong skills in classroom organization and management are more likely to be effective in helping teachers create productive learning environments. Experience in how to increase teaching time and establish routines and procedures that make the classroom a safe, orderly, and productive learning environment helps when working with teachers who want to increase their own expertise in these areas. Coaches can help teachers identify strategies that will lead to increased student engagement and on-task behavior.

Although coaches come to the role with teaching expertise, effective coaches continue to develop their content knowledge, pedagogical expertise, pedagogical content knowledge, and expertise in assessment as they coach so that they have an increased range of options for supporting teachers.

Coaching skills

Coaching has a greater effect if coaches are skilled in building teachers' capacity to be resourceful, make informed decisions, solve problems, and adapt to meet student learning needs. Coaches begin with an understanding of how adults learn and the stages of learning from novice to master teacher. The coach diagnoses teacher needs and determines the appropriate supports and interventions to address the teacher's needs. Coaches use their knowledge of the goals of the coaching program, various roles of coaches, strategies coaches use, and different models of coaching (such as Cognitive Coaching[SM], technical coaching, content coaching) to decide the most suitable coaching method to meet the teacher's needs and achieve the coaching program's goals.

Another core coaching skill is offering or providing support without judging a teacher's effectiveness or implying that the teacher's skills are inadequate. Florida researchers reported:

> While knowledge and experience appear to be central to teachers' perceptions of coach quality, the coach's style or approach to working with teachers was another attribute widely cited in case study visits. For example, several teachers at one school commended the coach for "offering help without pushing it" and showing teachers "another option rather than making it feel like you're doing something wrong." (Marsh et al., 2008, p. 64)

To help develop a teacher's expertise, an effective coach builds a relationship based on trust and respect. Effective coaches use communication skills that convey respect as they talk with teachers, such as pausing to allow time to formulate thoughtful responses, paraphrasing to clarify understanding, and questioning to promote deeper understanding and mine for information. Perhaps the most challenging and important communication skill that a coach can apply in order to be effective in his or her work is to listen with respect. Dennis Sparks describes committed listening as a type of listening that "allows the speaker to determine the agenda for what is said, seeks to understand the

speaker's views, is nonjudgmental, and honors the speaker's perspective" (2005, p. 52). In order to understand teachers' concerns, desires, and perspectives, coaches must learn to be good listeners.

Coaches use a variety of questioning skills to promote deeper understanding, probe for more information, and generate new ideas. Coaches encourage teachers to reflect on their practice by guiding them through a reflection process. A reflection process might be:

- Develop an understanding of one's actions and the responses they elicited. What happened in this particular situation or series of events?
- Analyze the responses. What are possible reasons for the responses?
- Generate a list of lessons learned from the analysis and past knowledge. How is this experience similar to past experiences? What are you learning from this experience?
- Apply the lessons in future situations. How might this lesson influence one's future actions?

Relationship skills

Effective coaches need good interpersonal relationships. The effective coach recognizes the power of collaboration and wants to be part of a team working toward common goals and managing issues productively. Effective coaches are less interested in being recognized for their own work than in having the team recognized for the work. Effective coaches understand the importance of establishing trust in their relationships and the importance of fostering trusting relationships across the school community, enabling them to work effectively with administrators and teachers. When trust exists between the coach and staff and between the principal and coach, the coach is more credible and more likely to have a positive influence on teacher practice and have peers' respect. Effective coaches are patient with the learning process because they understand adult learners' needs and the change process. They recognize that teachers need and want support to implement changes, and they are patient and persistent as teachers learn new practices. They create and nurture a learning environment that fosters collaboration within and across teams of teachers within the school community so teachers feel less isolated as they implement new strategies.

Content expertise

One pathway to improving student learning is to deepen teachers' content knowledge. Some coaches, particularly instructional coaches, may be challenged if they do not have expertise in various content areas. Coaches who are expected to support teachers in a single content area are more likely to be credible if they have experience teaching that content area and are offering support in the designated content only. On the other hand, coaches who are expected to work with teachers of all content areas face a greater challenge to know best practices within multiple content areas.

Coaches sometimes know that the best strategy when they do not have expertise in multiple content areas is to establish a collegial learning environment in which teachers are likely to learn with and from each other. Effective coaches then use strategies that engage teachers in reflecting on their practice using their own classroom data.

In either case, effective coaches keep their knowledge of best practices and content current. Coaches will find it particularly challenging to help teachers implement a curriculum they have not actually taught, so they must become and remain well versed in research-based instructional strategies, must actively learn about the curriculum, and must engage teachers in making sound decisions about curriculum and instruction to produce student results. The ability to help teachers understand the relationship between content knowledge,

the curriculum, and decisions about pedagogy enhances coaches' credibility with teachers and potentially leads to improved student performance.

Leadership skills

Coaches often do not have strong leadership skills in supporting adult learning (Marsh et al., 2008). Because coaching is essentially about professional learning, when coaches lack expertise about best practices in professional learning, their overall effectiveness is limited.

In addition to understanding effective professional learning, coaches apply skills in planning improvement efforts based on professional learning. They help individuals, teams, and the whole faculty:

- Set ambitious goals based on analyzing student, teacher, and school data;
- Identify indicators of success and benchmarks of progress;
- Plan professional learning needed to achieve the goals;
- Identify resources needed to accomplish the learning;
- Support implementation of classroom professional learning;
- Provide constructive feedback;
- Facilitate formative and summative assessments of progress toward the goal using student, educator, and school data; and
- Repeat the cycle.

As members of schoolwide committees, such as a school leadership team, coaches have opportunities to model how to set goals and monitor progress toward those goals for improved student learning. Coaches who step into leadership roles beyond their coaching role then model to other teachers the potential of teacher leadership and exert broader influence on the school's goals for teacher and student learning. Coaches' role as school leaders is essential in developing and maintaining a collaborative culture that results in productive decision making and problem solving to address teachers' ongoing challenges.

Effective coaches use data to influence teachers' decisions about their classroom practices. They continually communicate the school's vision and align their work with school goals. They help teachers develop individual and team goals aligned with the school's goals and align collective efforts so that the teachers' work is streamlined, seems less overwhelming because all are working to achieve the same results, and is complementary. Coaches' ability to see overall school needs, assess individual teacher needs based on data, and use data to make decisions contributes to their overall success.

Finally, skillful coaches demonstrate a working knowledge of transitions and how change occurs. They understand that change is a process that takes time, and that individuals have stages of concern and experience different levels of use as they are expected to work in new and different ways. To help teachers manage change and improve their practice, coaches work with teachers to develop benchmarks and indicators of success. Since those who experience change respond in different ways, coaches have a repertoire of strategies to respond with so that they maintain a positive, supportive, and trusting relationship with teachers. Effective coaches apply research about change, such as the Concerns Based Adoption Model (CBAM), to understand teachers' feelings and address their concerns. Research, theories, or models about change provide the coach a framework or roadmap from which to understand, support, and respond to teachers as they experience change.

Context

Coaches bring a wide range of beliefs, knowledge, skills, and expertise. Yet school conditions influence how effective the coach is. If trust among the staff and between the staff and school administrators is weak, teachers may be less likely to focus on their own continuous improvement and more likely to resist working with a coach. When coaches and teachers don't have adequate time to collaborate, teachers may be less responsive to the opportunity to be coached. If staff members' beliefs interfere with their own or students' capacity to learn, even the most skillful coach is likely to meet with resistance. If staff members do not understand the coach's role within the school, they may generate their own unhealthy explanations for coaching.

On the other hand, if the school schedule, values and goals, expectations for students and staff, and sense of collective responsibility support continuous improvement, a coach, even a novice coach, is likely to succeed.

Effective coaches use data to influence teachers' decisions about their classroom practices.

How teachers and principals perceive the quality of their coach influences the coach's work and its impact. Researchers have found a strong correlation between teachers' assessment of the quality of coaching they received and their perceptions of coaching's effects on their instruction (Marsh et al., 2008). In addition, principals' assessment of the coach's ability to support adult learners was positively associated with teachers' and principals' perceptions of coaches' influence (Marsh et al., 2008). What this means is that coaching works best in schools where the staff understand the purpose of coaching, the coach is well prepared for his role; the coach exhibits skillfulness in his interactions with staff members; and the principal has confidence in the coach's abilities to serve in the role.

Scenario

Angelique Iyer has been a middle school instructional coach in her small district for the last three years. She was a science teacher in the same school before becoming a coach.

Her transition into her new role went smoothly because she was a masterful, well-respected teacher and because she had extensive training that positioned her to be successful from the start. Both her immediate supervisor — the school's assistant principal — and the teachers she works with report she has been supportive and has contributed to their professional learning. Although the district is small, the leadership team wanted all of the new coaches to have training to prepare them for their work. The district arranged for Iyer and her colleagues throughout the district to take part in a six-day district coaching institute during the summer before they started in the role. Iyer learned the importance of establishing trust with her principal and teachers so they would be more receptive to working with her. She took a deliberate and thoughtful approach to building trust in her new role. She made sure to follow through with her commitments, worked on her communication skills, took care not to convey judgment about teachers' practices, was a good listener, and regularly asked teachers' opinions.

Iyer hoped that her colleagues would recognize that she knew about effective instruction and that though she had taught science, would recognize that she knew how to use curriculum guides; how to design effective instruction, assessments, and learning tasks to engage students; and how to build learning communities within classrooms. She wanted to work as a partner with her colleagues, not as an expert, so she repeatedly reminded them that the coach's role is to support teachers, not to evaluate or supervise them.

During the first few months in her new role, Iyer listened more than she talked. She asked teachers to describe their successes and challenges with student learning. She invited them to identify students whom they wanted to succeed who were not meeting expectations. She engaged teachers in collaborative teams to look at student data.

After the first few months, however, Iyer felt she needed to do more to focus on effective instruction in all disciplines, particularly to engage students more actively in the learning process. Through this time, most of her work was with teacher teams, meeting during common planning periods to facilitate teacher conversations about assessment data. Iyer worked with a few teachers individually, and their feedback to the principal was positive.

In her weekly conversation with the principal and assistant principal, Iyer asked to have time at the following two faculty meetings to help staff examine student classroom engagement. She selected three articles on the role of active student engagement in learning and assigned each teacher one of the articles to read before the faculty meeting. She then prepared several questions related to each article to guide the staff's discussion.

At the two meetings, Iyer facilitated whole-faculty, small-group, grade-level, and subject-specific conversations about the articles and the implications for teaching and learning in the school. At the second meeting, Iyer asked staff members to identify strategies for engaging students and to identify what each department would do to improve student engagement. After the second faculty meeting, she provided mini-lessons to each department on using different strategies aligned with their lessons and disciplines to engage students.

In a subsequent meeting with the principal and assistant principal, Iyer asked for help in thinking about how to assess whether student engagement was increasing and whether the emphasis on engagement affected student achievement. She wanted to help teachers know that their efforts affected student academic success.

Reflection questions

- What characteristics of an effective coach did Iyer exhibit? Which would you characterize as strengths and which might be areas of focus for further development?

- How does Iyer's preparation to become a coach compare with your own? In considering Iyer's actions in the first few months of the school year, what do you think was emphasized in her preparation?

- Iyer made some assumptions about how to begin work as a coach. What were some of her assumptions, and how do they align with the characteristics of effective coaches?

- Iyer met frequently with the principal and assistant principal. How did those meetings support her as a coach and help her continue to develop her expertise?

- Iyer acknowledged she didn't know everything she wanted to know about coaching for instructional improvement and sought assistance to fill those gaps. Using the characteristics of effective school-based coaches in Table 3.1, identify your own strengths as a coach and some areas for growth. How will you get support to improve your coaching practice?

Central office administrators

- Set clear expectations for the coach's roles and responsibilities.

- Provide or help provide professional learning to allow coaches to become more effective in all facets of their role.

- Give coaches opportunities to assess themselves on the degree to which they possess the characteristics of effective coaches.

- Create a coach evaluation aligned with the goals of the coaching program, expectations for coaches' work, and the criteria for effectiveness.

- Give coaches a format to set goals in each of the areas of effectiveness and allow them to monitor their progress over time.

- Offer coaches opportunities to network with and learn from each other.

Building administrators

- Help the coach set goals for professional growth based on the characteristics of effective coaches.

- Meet regularly with the coach to help monitor progress on his or her professional growth plan.

- Support the coach in accomplishing the coach's professional growth plan goals.

- Provide opportunities for the coach to engage in professional learning related to his or her professional goals.

Coaches

- Develop awareness of the characteristics of an effective coach.

- Conduct a self-assessment of the skills, knowledge, and attitudes needed to be an effective coach.

- Solicit the principal's and teachers' feedback on your strengths and areas for growth.

- Establish formal goals for professional growth related to the characteristics of an effective coach, and monitor your progress over time.

- Seek multiple opportunities to enhance the skills and knowledge you need to become more effective as a coach.

Recommendations for

TOOL INDEX
Chapter 3

	TOOL	PURPOSE
3.1	**Instructional coach professional development plan**	Use this tool as a coach to set goals and action plans for professional growth related to student achievement.
3.2	**Instructional coach self-assessment**	Assess your strengths and areas of need as a coach in relation to the attributes of effective coaches.
3.3	**Instructional coach self-assessment activity**	Assess your strengths and areas of need as a coach in relation to the attributes of effective coaches using a Likert scale.
3.4	**Principles we live by**	Follow this process to examine your principles and beliefs about your work as an instructional coach.

To download tools, see www.learningforward.org/publications/coachingmatters

Types
of coaching

Despite the prevalence of coaching in schools and districts, there is no standard model or uniform definition of an instructional coach, nor are there standard ways of selecting, preparing, deploying, supporting, or evaluating coaches. This might seem problematic on the surface, particularly to researchers striving to measure coaching's effect on teaching and student learning. Whether this inconsistency creates challenges depends on what education reformers assume about how to create change in schools. Standardization is easier to implement with fidelity and apply broadly. Adaptation, however, allows more personalization to address specific and disparate needs. Resolving this debate is not the purpose of this book.

Instead, school and district leaders and coaches themselves can review various models of coaching to understand the breadth of options, to bring into sharper focus the distinctions that exist among some of the approaches, and to deliberate about the best approach for their own context and desired results. While some approaches may fit better, the real determinant of "best fit" is the result.

To make a decision about an approach to coaching, ask:

- What problem are we trying to address?
- What are the root causes of the identified needs?
- What other means have we considered to address the problem?
- What evidence points to coaching as the best intervention in this situation?
- What resources are available to support implementing and maintaining a coaching program?

For coaches and coaching to be successful, it is important to be clear about what type of coaching will be offered.

Once leaders have decided to explore coaching, those deciding what to implement can consider what type or types of coaching are most appropriate to achieve the intended results. Some argue that all approaches to coaching are similar; many approaches build on a common knowledge base, use similar skill sets, rest on common assumptions, and encompass similar practices. Others might find approaches they say are better, more evidence-based, and more effective. Research-based evidence is not available to declare a winner in this debate.

Five models of coaching

Not all coaching is the same. Some coaches focus on instructional improvements in all disciplines. Some focus only on particular disciplines. For coaches and coaching to be successful, it is important to be clear about what type of coaching will be offered and how well the type of coaching aligns with the coaching program's goals for teacher and student learning. A summary of these models appears in Table 4.1.

Instructional coaching

According to Barry W. Sweeny, "Instructional coaches customize professional development to match each teacher's needs and interests while they help the school establish a common understanding across all teachers" (2001, p. 50).

Instructional coaches demonstrate lessons, co-plan lessons with teachers or teams, and co-teach to help teachers grow professionally and learn new strategies. They help teachers plan instruction and assessment, solve problems, and reflect.

Although instructional coaches consult, collaborate, and reflect, their primary responsibility is to reflect with teachers and provide nonjudgmental support. Instructional coaches follow a gradual release model (I do, we do, you do) in order to transition out of the classroom supporter role and into the role of reflective coach.

A reflective coach helps a teacher reflect on teaching before, during, and after a lesson to help the teacher improve decisions about instruction. The instructional coach engages teachers in learning-focused conversations that generate insights about their professional practice.

Instructional coaches have expertise in pedagogy and effective instructional strategies.

Technical coaching

Technical coaching, according to Robert Garmston, "helps teachers transfer training to classroom practice. It generally follows training in specific teaching methods: this model pairs consultants with teachers or teachers with one another" (1987, p. 18).

Coaches use a technical coaching model when they need to provide specific information about how to do something, give advice, or solve a problem. The coach's focus is on helping teachers acquire logistical information or pedagogical or content knowledge.

Technical coaching is an appropriate choice when the goal is to ensure a level of fidelity to a program. For example, the coach might count how many times a teacher asks a class a higher-order question, might share that information with the teacher, and then might analyze the questions to work with the teacher to turn more of the teacher's queries into higher-level questions. Technical coaches have been integral to helping teachers implement Success for All and Reading Recovery programs.

Technical coaches are expert providers of resources, or help teachers access them, and have expertise in demonstrating or modeling teaching.

Content coaching

Content coaches support teachers and offer feedback in a content area, typically literacy or mathematics. They base their work on grade-level standards, curriculum and content expectations, and data related to instruction and student learning. Content coaches help teachers design lessons that incorporate big ideas and require skilled teaching. They help teachers analyze and reflect on lessons. Their goal is to provide teachers with a set of instructional tools for designing lessons and assessing students' content area skills.

Like technical coaches, content coaches need expertise in their content area. Unlike technical coaches, however, their work most often is not directed by any particular program or methodology. However, they may support teachers' efforts to implement a program focused on a content area.

According to Lucy West (2009, p. 115), the two goals of content coaching are to cultivate teachers' academic habits of reasoning and discourse associated with a particular discipline and to help teachers develop a set of skills that will enable them to cultivate those habits in their students, habits that will promote student appreciation and understanding of the subject at hand.

Content coaches have content expertise.

Cognitive coaching

Arthur Costa and Garmston (2002) developed the cognitive coaching process in 1984. Cognitive Coaching is based on the belief that clients have internal resources and their own best answers. The coach's goal is to reflect clients' thinking back to them, helping them to find their own way. A metaphor is the coach as a mirror, reflecting thinking back to the client.

Cognitive coaches strive to build teachers' internal resources and capacities by using intentional communication skills, including paraphrasing and probing. Rather than giving teachers evaluative feedback, coaches focus on supporting clients to become conscious of their actions and the impact of their actions on learners.

Costa and Garmston (2002, p. 5) assert that cognitive coaching — with its model of planning, reflecting, and solving problems — is at the heart of professional communities that "honor autonomy, encourage interdependence, and produce high achievement." One distinction of this type of coaching is that the coach does not need to have more expertise in a content area than the client in order to be effective in this role.

Cognitive coaches have expertise in developing habits of mind and the cognitive aspects of teaching.

Peer coaching

Peer coaching requires that each person act as the coach and as the client at different times. Sheila Valencia and Joellen Killion define peer coaching as "a process where teams of teachers regularly observe one another and provide support companionship, feedback, and assistance" (1988, p. 170). Peer coaching is appropriate when two or more teachers want to collaborate in order to improve their instruction.

This type of coaching depends on and helps build a collaborative culture in which stakeholders value adult learning. Those who participate in peer coaching may or may not have greater expertise than their peers, but all make clear their intent to learn from each other.

Peer coaches have expertise in collaboration and inquiry.

While various types of coaching share similarities, each has its own purposes. A lack of clarity about which coaching model is being used or combining multiple models without being clear about their purposes and use leads to confusion and complicates practice.

Table 4.1 Overall considerations of coaching models

COACHING MODEL	DESCRIPTION	GOAL	WHEN TO USE	CONSIDERATIONS
Instructional coaching	**Expertise:** Pedagogy and effective instructional strategies. **Recipient:** Those who teach students or adults a wide variety of subjects or teach skills in broader areas such as instructional strategies, concepts, pedagogy, theory, etc. **Provider:** An expert or master teacher/instructor in numerous areas, including pedagogy and theory.	To increase teacher effectiveness and student learning by supporting teachers in implementing proven practices, reflecting on their instructional decisions, and making needed adjustments.	When there is a gap between teachers' knowledge and their implementation of instructional strategies, and student learning results could improve.	Coaches help teachers identify their ideal classroom and support and guide them in achieving that goal. They help identify teaching practices that will help teachers realize their goals. The coach becomes a "thinking partner" with the teacher.

Table 4.1 Overall considerations of coaching models (cont'd)

COACHING MODEL	DESCRIPTION	GOAL	WHEN TO USE	CONSIDERATIONS
Content coaching	**Expertise:** Content. **Recipient:** Those working in a targeted academic subject or content area (for example, reading, math, science). **Provider:** An expert or master in the content area.	To increase teacher effectiveness and student learning by focusing on improving content knowledge and skills.	When teachers need content specific support to learn curriculum, assessment strategies, or pedagogy.	Content coaches may have more credibility with clients because of their content expertise. Content coaches may be more limited in their ability to work with teachers across multiple content areas, and their overall potential to affect schoolwide practices may be limited.
Technical coaching	**Expertise:** Providing resources or helping to access them; ability to demonstrate or model teaching. **Recipient:** Those needing information or advice about content or skills. (The technical coach advocates for particular actions or choices.) **Provider:** Information specialists able to clarify, model, provide data, and make suggestions.	To increase teacher effectiveness and student learning by improving knowledge of processes, procedures, resources, and protocols.	When the client needs support to be more self-directed.	The client may become dependent on the technical coach for advice and confirmation about decisions and actions. This type of coaching requires a high level of trust and strong relationships so that clients feel honored for the knowledge and skills they possess.

Table 4.1 Overall considerations of coaching models (cont'd)

COACHING MODEL	DESCRIPTION	GOAL	WHEN TO USE	CONSIDERATIONS
Cognitive Coaching	**Expertise**: Knowledge of developing habits of mind and the cognitive aspects of teaching. **Recipient:** Those developing the cognitive aspects of teaching. **Provider:** Someone trained in Cognitive Coaching.	To increase teacher effectiveness and student learning by developing the teacher's ability to make intentional instructional decisions and to reflect and learn from those decisions.	When masterful teachers want to improve or teachers demonstrate a need to improve.	Clients who lack "internal resources" about content or pedagogy, such as novice teachers, may benefit from a more direct type of coaching.
Peer coaching	**Expertise:** Skilled in collaboration and inquiry. **Recipient and provider:** Peers work together to support each other by observing one another and providing feedback.	To increase teacher effectiveness and student learning by providing opportunities for co-learning about effective instruction.	When two or more colleagues wish to collaborate in order to improve their knowledge and skills about instruction.	Peer collaboration involves co-pondering and co-learning. Without a perceived expert, all participants have equal responsibility to act as coach and client (at different times). This type of coaching can help reduce teacher isolation, make effective teaching strategies more transparent, and support the habit of reflective practice.

Commonalities of coaching models

Although each coaching model has distinct characteristics, all share some commonalities. Each coaching model shares a focus on close, sustained connections to teachers' daily classroom work and problems of practice and a purpose of improving student learning by facilitating teacher development. In all models, successful coaching partnerships are based on high levels of trust and relationships, and coaching is not evaluative.

The research on school-based coaches, including research by Richard Elmore (1996) and Bruce Joyce and Beverly Showers (1995), supports coaching and finds that teachers implement new instructional practices much more frequently when they have been coached. (See Table 4.2.)

Joyce and Showers have shown that the transfer rate — the frequency with which new learning actually is used in the classroom — is low when teacher learning is from presentations or even demonstrations. The researchers' work stems from their hypothesis that initial training followed by coaching results in much higher levels of transfer than when teachers experience training alone. Joyce and Showers proved this hypothesis initially in 1980 and again in subsequent studies.

Those distinguishing among coaching models typically look at coaching practices. A higher level offers distinctive approaches to coaching that consider the coach's content, processes, and drive. These distinctions are another way to think about coaching models. They can be grouped to focus on four areas: content or process, people or results, action or metacognition, and correction or continuous improvement.

Content or process

In this coaching approach, the coach focuses on subject-specific or pedagogy-specific interactions with the client. The coach addresses literacy, math, science, or other disciplines or focuses on formative assessment, active engagement, classroom behaviors, or other pedagogical processes. However, to coach science, the coach also must coach how science is taught, and the divide between content and process ceases to exist.

Person or results

Another approach focuses on the clients whom the coach serves. For example, mentors support novice teachers who often are in their first through third year of teaching. Others coach teachers at any point in their career development. Because results are impossible without a focus on the person, person-focused coaching and results-focused coaching are intertwined. In practice, though, the division is clearer.

Few coaches are prepared early in their careers to work with teachers to unpack the assumptions that are barriers to changing practice. Coaches more often are trained in communication skills and strategies and how to build trusting relationships. The kind of conversations that change both assumptions and practice also challenge mental models.

An emphasis on relationship as coaching's primary goal means that results often are slow to occur. Expert coaches know how to navigate challenging conversations so that they can bring to the surface teachers' assumptions that impede practice. When coaches shift their priority from forming relationships to producing results for students, their work is more effective.

Action or metacognition

Another distinction that some propose is action and metacognition. Action-focused coaching is based on the idea that there is a set of research- and evidence-based behaviors or practices that distinguish effective teaching from less effective

Table 4.2 Relationship between training components and impact on teachers

TRAINING COMPONENTS	Understand knowledge and skills impact on teachers	Actually learn skills	Actually apply skills in the classroom
Presentation of theory	85%	15%	5%-10%
Modeling	85%	18%	5%-10%
Practice and low-risk feedback	85%	80%	10%-15%
Coaching feedback and peer visits	90%	90%	80%-90%

Source: Joyce, B. & Showers, B. (1995). *Student achievement through staff development: Fundamentals of school renewal.* White Plains, NY: Longman.

teaching. Further, coaching teachers to use more of the research- and evidence-based practices will result in more successful students. As districts and states shape educator effectiveness systems, they are culling these practices from decades of research and existing frameworks and incorpo-

> Coaching teachers to use more of the research- and evidence-based practices will result in more successful students.

rating the practices into teaching and learning frameworks, performance standards, and evaluation criteria. Examples of such frameworks related to teaching include Charlotte Danielson's Framework of Teaching (2007) and CLASS™

(Classroom Assessment Scoring System, Teachstone Training, 2012), which is the basis for many district and state educator effectiveness systems.

Metacognition-focused coaching, which is based on cognitive psychology, emphasizes mental models as drivers. Metacognition-focused coaching helps teachers examine their underlying beliefs in an effort to change the way they carry out instruction. Metacognition-focused coaching helps teachers discern cues that trigger a need to change their practice and then make decisions about how to do so. Tied to the work of Donald Schoen, Penelope Peterson, and others who examined reflection and teacher decision making, metacognition-focused coaching emphasizes how people make decisions about what actions to take, the influences on those decisions, and being conscious of one's internal thought processes.

Correction or continuous improvement

Sometimes coaching works to correct teaching practice; other times it is a means to continuous, career-long development. In the first approach, correction, coaching is based on the assumption that current teaching practices are inadequate or not at the desired performance level, as in the case of a teacher not performing at proficiency level according to a defined performance evaluation system. Coaching might be one intervention to help support the teacher and give the teacher opportunities to improve his or her competency to be able to meet the expected standard of practice. In this approach to coaching, the client and coach have a common goal — to improve performance to meet the standards. Coaches may have more liberty to be directive, especially if the teacher is motivated or faces an urgent need to improve. Directive strategies might include advising, suggesting improvements, or giving specific direction about strategies to use. Correction-focused coaching often is mandatory rather than voluntary, which changes the dynamic of the coach-client relationship. Coaches who have knowledge and experience in the practices that the teacher needs to improve most often provide this coaching.

The second approach, continuous improvement-focused coaching, acknowledges that professionals are responsible for refining and expanding their professional practice throughout their careers and that they do so by setting and achieving personal and professional improvement goals, engaging in purposeful professional learning, reflecting privately and publicly, and seeking and using feedback from peers, subordinates, and supervisors. Continuous improvement-focused coaching offers an opportunity to receive feedback, examine potential improvements, and seek support to make those improvements. Continuous improvement-focused coaching may occur periodically throughout an educator's career, may be more consistent, and may be voluntary or required. Peers, supervisors, and knowledgeable others can provide continuous improvement-focused coaching. The scope and type of improvement sought may help determine the person best suited to coach. When the intended improvement is significant and requires specialized knowledge and skills, such as when a person moves into a new position, a knowledgeable other person may be the best coach.

> The very best coaches are those who are able to adjust their approach to coaching to meet the needs of a particular situation, the client, and the program's intended outcome.

Commonalities across types

Distinguishing among types of coaching brings into focus how coaches serve teachers, the specific expertise they need to succeed in their roles, and the focus for their initial and ongoing professional learning. Those who lead coaching programs understand that the very best coaches are those who are able to adjust their approach to coaching to meet the needs of a particular situation, the client, and the program's intended outcome. Effective leaders support coaches with their own professional learning for all models and work to help the coaches understand how different models can be woven together to form a tapestry of skills and strategies that support coaches' success.

Scenario

As the Bradford School District introduced its new literacy program for students in 3rd through 10th grades, the literacy coordinator and principals were acutely aware that the program's ability to increase student reading performance depended on how well teachers understood how students become proficient in literacy, how well teachers implemented the program, and how teachers adapted literacy lessons and experiences to meet students' individual learning needs. Because the new program was significantly different from the previous one, the literacy coordinator asked that the district hire coaches to help expand teachers' content expertise in the district's lowest-performing schools.

After district staff conducted an extensive study of the effects of coaching and analyzed ways to fund the additional positions, the school board approved enough new positions for the district to place a full-time literacy coach in each school whose students performed below the district mean. This meant that almost half of the elementary schools, all the middle schools, and each high school would get coaches. The coaching positions were a significant investment.

After developing criteria for selecting coaches, principals hired coaches for their school. The literacy coordinator provided extensive training for the coaches so they understood how to support teachers in implementing the new literacy program. The coaches responded on feedback forms that they appreciated the training and were ready and eager to begin their new jobs.

Within a few weeks, however, coaches, teachers, and principals recognized that classroom cultures and student work habits were presenting unexpected challenges that interfered with the coaches' purpose of supporting teacher implementation of the new literacy program. Although the coaches and teachers had good intentions and the teachers seemed willing to implement the new content, the coaches found that student engagement was low and that ensuing discipline issues were regularly interfering. Teacher and student attitudes began to sour, and coaches became frustrated with the lack of progress.

The literacy coordinator called a meeting with teacher representatives, principals, and coaches to discuss the identified challenges and to plan how to address them. As a result of their meeting, the literacy coordinator temporarily shifted the coach role from literacy coaches who supported implementation of the literacy program to instructional coaches to help teachers develop classroom routines, work with student behavior, and develop flexible and cooperative environments in each classroom.

Reflection questions

- What was the intended type of coaching in Bradford School District? What factors contributed to the district selecting that type of coaching?

- How might the type of coaching have been decided to best meet the district's needs?

- What factors might the district have considered in making the change to the type of coaching offered?

- How will coaches know when they are able to switch from their roles as instructional coaches back to coaching literacy?

- Considering the experience of coaches in Bradford School District, how does knowing about the types of coaches help coaches and district and school leaders meet teacher needs?

Recommendations for

Central office administrators

- Identify the coaching model that best matches district goals or the features of each model that align with the coaching program design and goals.
- Consider available resources when selecting coaching models.
- Clarify expectations and desired outcomes for the coaches' work.
- Design professional learning for coaches in the desired model of coaching.
- Decide whether to employ external coaching consultants to build internal capacity.
- Be specific about how much leeway coaches have to implement more than one coaching model or to use skills more commonly associated with a specific coaching model.
- Use the description of coaching models and their distinctions to clarify how coaching will operate in the district. Consider needed changes.
- Use the models of coaching and the distinctions to engage coaches in examining their practice.

Building administrators

- Align partnership agreements with the elements of the coaching model used in the school and district.
- Communicate clear expectations to the staff about the coaching model and how it affects the coach's work.
- Clarify misunderstandings about the coaching model used in the school or district.
- Respond to questions about the particular coaching model.
- Clarify for staff what latitude coaches have to use more than one coaching model.

Coaches

- Develop partnership agreements with the principal and teachers that align closely to the coaching model being used.
- Explain the rationale for the coaching model being used and emphasize how the model affects the types of services provided.
- Ensure that teachers have voice and choice in how to work with the coach.
- Maintain the integrity of the selected coaching model.
- Understand how much variance is acceptable in implementing the coaching model.
- Talk with supervisors about challenges with the particular coaching model being used, and suggest ways to address those challenges.
- Seek feedback on the coaching model from teachers and supervisors.
- Use the coaching models and distinctions chart to examine your practice, find examples of behaviors you have used that align with multiple models, and consider how your current beliefs align with the distinctions described.

TOOL INDEX
Chapter 4

	TOOL	PURPOSE
4.1	**Relationship between training outcomes and training components**	Use this tool to demonstrate the impact of coaching on teachers' practices.
4.2	**Coaching interactions**	Gain an understanding of the range of coaching stances with this visual depiction.
4.3	**Instructional conversation protocol**	Adapt for your own situation this example of an instructional conversation protocol that an instructional coach might use.
4.4	**Classroom observation checklist**	Provide technical coaching about specific instructional practices using a checklist such as this one.
4.5	**Peer observation protocol**	Focus a conversation based on a peer observation using this protocol.
4.6	**Instructional planning template**	Use this template as a planning tool before meeting with your coach, or as a coach, use the template as a guide for planning lessons with teachers.

To download tools, see www.learningforward.org/publications/coachingmatters

Roles
of coaches

Effective programs clearly define the coach's roles. They define what results the district wants from coaching, and they focus coaches' work on a few, high-leverage roles that will achieve the intended results.

When coaching programs lack clear role definitions, coaches' work is not substantive enough to produce any results. In many schools, coaches already are perceived as and perceive themselves as jacks-of-all-trades. They often are scattered, pulled in many directions trying to serve teachers' disparate needs without any parameters. Unable to prepare, they end up having limited influence on teaching and learning. Some coaching programs have been eliminated because teachers, coaches, and principals are uncertain about what the coach's role is, and so they fail to demonstrate that coaches are effective in improving teaching and student learning.

Research and evaluations find that focusing coaches' work is one feature of successful coaching programs. An evaluation in the Poudre (Colo.) School District found that "at sites where principals communicated about the roles and responsibilities of the coach with the staff on an ongoing basis … coaches experienced less resistance from teachers and felt more productive in their coaching" (2010, p. 5).

A 2008 RAND Corporation study (Marsh et al., 2008) of literacy and reading coaches in middle schools in Florida found that coaches' work typically is spread among many activities, including one-on-one work with teachers, informal work with teachers, coaching-related administrative duties, and noncoaching duties. The study found that some coaches' time was used in assessment management and administration, managing literacy materials (including ordering, budgeting, inventory, and locating and distributing resources), and placing students. Although coaches spent more time working one-on-one with teachers, the time amounted to less than half of their coaching work, the study found. Overall, the RAND study concluded, coaching had mixed results in its effect on student achievement, with small, yet significant results evident in two of the four cohorts of students studied.

A key finding in the Florida study was the difference in how coaches spent their time in low-performing and high-performing schools. In higher performing schools, coaches spent less time assessing students and less time managing resources (Marsh et al., 2008).

Another important finding in the Florida study was the difference between inexperienced and experienced coaches' activities. While both made individual instructional activities with teachers a priority, experienced coaches spent more time with teachers analyzing and using data than did their less-experienced counterparts.

The fundamental focus of a coach's work influences the potential of a coaching program to produce results. When district and school leaders set the program's parameters and consider what work coaches are expected to do each day, coaches have the greatest leverage to improve teaching and student learning.

10 roles and responsibilities of coaches

Joellen Killion and Cindy Harrison (2006) identify 10 possible roles for coaches: resource provider, data coach, instructional specialist, curriculum specialist, classroom supporter, learning facilitator, mentor, school leader, catalyst for change, and learner. Each role is distinct, yet roles frequently overlap to provide teachers with rich and deep support.

- **Resource provider.** Coaches help colleagues by sharing classroom-focused instructional resources. Resources might include website addresses, instructional materials, leveled books, or materials to use with students. Coaches also might share professional resources, such as articles, books, lesson or unit plans, and assessment tools.

- **Data coach.** Although teachers have access to a great deal of data, they often do not use the available data to make decisions about classroom instruction. Coaches can lead conversations that engage teachers in analyzing and using a variety of data to strengthen instruction.

- **Instructional specialist.** As instructional specialists, coaches help colleagues implement effective teaching strategies. They might share ideas for differentiating instruction or planning lessons in partnership with fellow teachers; share research-based classroom strategies (Marzano, Pickering, & Pollock, 2001); explore which instructional methodologies are appropriate for particular curricula; and develop teachers' capacity in instructional areas such as designing and implementing formative assessments, increasing student engagement, or increasing students' application of higher-level thinking skills in classroom work.

- **Curriculum specialist.** Effective teachers understand content standards such as the Common Core State Standards, and they know how to use these standards to plan instruction. As curriculum specialists, coaches model how to use standards to plan instruction and assessment. They help teachers to use common pacing charts and develop shared assessments. They help teachers understand and integrate curricula across disciplines to reinforce learning outcomes. They build consistency and coherence across classrooms, grade levels, courses, and schools to ensure that the curriculum is implemented consistently throughout a school and district.

- **Classroom supporter.** Classroom supporters work inside classrooms to help teachers implement new ideas. They often demonstrate a lesson, co-teach, or observe and give feedback. As classroom supporters, coaches work to enhance teachers' efficacy and improve teaching. Whether the coach models, co-plans a lesson and co-teaches, or observes the teacher, the coach and teacher spend time preparing and debriefing their joint work. Coaches strive to raise teachers' consciousness and skillfulness about making decisions that lead to successful instruction.

- **Learning facilitator.** This coaching role creates opportunities for and facilitates professional learning among staff members. When teachers learn with and from one another, they focus on professional learning that most directly affects student learning. Their professional learning becomes more relevant, is linked to their day-to-day classroom work, and aligns with identified goals for student learning. When coaches bring teachers together in communities of learners who share goals for student success, they can break down norms of isolation that exist among teachers in many schools and begin to rebuild cultures of collaboration and collective responsibility.

- **Mentor.** A common role for coaches in schools is to mentor novice teachers. Mentors are role models, acculturate new teachers to the school, and advise new teachers about instruction, curriculum, procedures, practices, and school politics. As a mentor, a coach may use any of the 10 identified roles to help a novice become an expert professional. The advantage of coaches serving as mentors is their ability to integrate novice teachers into the schoolwide community for professional learning rather than isolating them and fostering collective support to develop and acclimate novice teachers. In this way, the novice sees models of what more experienced teachers do, fully engages in all aspects of a teacher's work, and more quickly advances as a professional.

- **School leader.** Being a school leader means serving on a committee, such as a school improvement team; acting as a grade-level or department chair; supporting school initiatives; or representing the school on community or districtwide task forces or committees. School leaders share the school vision, align their professional goals with school and district goals, and share responsibility for the school's overall success. Because coaches are naturally leaders among their peers, taking on a more formal role as a school leader gives more opportunities to model teacher leadership and make their work transparent to others who want opportunities to lead.

- **Catalyst for change.** Coaches also can be catalysts for change, visionaries who are "never content with the status quo but rather always looking for a better way" (Lamel, 2007, p. 32). Coaches who become catalysts for change feel secure in their own work and are committed to continual improvement. They prompt teachers to analyze student learning, question the status quo, engage others in exploring possibilities, and identify the undiscussables within a school.

- **Learner.** One of the most important roles a coach can assume is that of learner. Learners model continual improvement, reflect on their work by seeking and graciously receiving feedback, experiment with new ideas, and use what they learn to help all teachers and students achieve. Because coaches' primary purpose is to support student achievement by improving teaching, coaches' work is fundamentally about engaging teachers in learning. By modeling their own learning, coaches send a powerful message about the importance of ongoing professional learning for increasing student achievement.

Narrow coaches' roles

Coaches cannot successfully perform all 10 roles, so narrowing expectations to a few roles increases the likelihood that they will be able to help teachers achieve results. District and school leaders use program goals to decide which coaching roles are most likely to be highest leverage for the district — looking at those most closely aligned to the program's intended outcomes.

For example, if the school's goal is to increase student performance in mathematics, selecting the roles of curriculum and instructional specialists and classroom supporter may be more advantageous for supporting the curriculum and instructional shifts necessary to increase student achievement. Roles such as school leader, mentor, and resource provider may be less influential in increasing student achievement. After determining which role is most appropriate, district and school leaders will need to conduct a deep analysis of the factors contributing to the problem and needed interventions.

Defining coaches' roles at the outset helps coaches, teachers, and supervisors understand what to expect. Left to themselves, coaches often find it easier to start as resource providers to build

credibility with teachers and gain entrée to classrooms, but they take the role with the least potential to affect student achievement. They may then move on to another role, such as instructional specialist, with more potential to affect student achievement. A well-defined role takes the guesswork out of the process and enables coaches to do their work more efficiently at the outset.

One principal stated, "There has been more movement in the last three months with a full-time coach whose job is well defined in the building than I saw in all the past 10 years put together" (Harrison, Clifton, & Bryan, 2010, p. 18).

One of the greatest challenges program designers face is identifying who makes the decision about coaches' roles. Principals may need to coordinate the work of multiple resource staff to ensure their work is aligned and not competing. Principals and teachers also sometimes believe they should decide what coaches do so that the coach meets the school's needs. However, if schools vary significantly in their needs, a coach who is successful in one school may not succeed in another, or may not even have the same qualifications as coaches in other schools. District-level staff may want to consider how coaches can be evaluated consistently districtwide, and how to invest in professional learning for coaches that will allow them to serve in more than one specific school.

Decision makers also need to consider what a reasonable workload is for coaches so that coaches start their job with the maximum potential for meeting expectations. District and school leaders can support coaches by being specific about how to spend their time. Coaches generally learn with experience how to allocate their time to roles that have the most influence on teaching practices. Providing coaches with guidelines for time allocations helps them adjust how they allot their time to their roles earlier and helps them avoid poor judgment or resorting to the roles that feel most comfortable.

Coaches, their supervisors, and the coach champion support the decisions about which roles to focus on and how to allot time by regularly monitoring how the coach is using time. Decision makers may specify the approximate percentages of time coaches should spend in particular roles and have regular conversations with the coaches about the desired percentages and actual time spent. Analyzing coaches' logs is one way to review how coaches allocate their time and consider what challenges interfere with their work.

Ongoing analysis of coaches' work includes not only the decisions coaches make about using their time, but also who and what influence their decisions. Sometimes individual building principals have an agenda and set priorities for their coaches' work that differ from the district's priorities. Some teachers' individual needs stretch coaches too thin, and coaches' work becomes too shallow to make a difference. Sometimes increasing responsibilities result from too many district initiatives adding to the coaches' workload, making it difficult for them to meet all their responsibilities.

In a Florida study (Marsh et al., 2008), coaches and principals identified barriers to coaches' work, including the number of teachers coaches work with, teachers lacking time in their schedules to work with their coaches, teacher reluctance to work with a coach, and coaches spending time on non-coaching assignments. When coaches, principals, and the coach champion identify barriers, they are able to more quickly find ways around them.

Balancing coaches' work with their need for ongoing professional learning presents another challenge. When coaches are away from their schools too often, teachers and principals alike wonder if coaches are meeting their role expectations.

However, coaches need time for extended professional learning and support to gain the specific knowledge and skills associated with each role. Some roles require knowledge and skills that are different

from effective teaching skills. Killion and Harrison (2006) identify the essential knowledge and skills associated with each of the 10 coaching roles.

The coach's job description offers one framework for defining the specifics of coaches' roles. Job descriptions help those interested in becoming coaches and those in coaching roles understand the school's or district's expectations. Job descriptions also are important tools for developing criteria used to evaluate coaches' effectiveness and provide coaches with feedback about their work. In the first year of a new program, limiting the number of roles coaches perform gives coaches time to prepare and establish productive relationships with teachers.

The coach's relationships also are strengthened when everyone involved has a clear picture of the coach's roles and responsibilities. Principals and the district staff who oversee the coaching program are responsible for introducing the coach's roles. All staff, and in particular those in schools, need to know what the coach does. Teachers often do not know exactly what coaches do, according to their comments from evaluations and audits of coaching programs. Teachers often are unclear about coaches' work when coaches have different roles in different schools and teachers compare the coaches' work across schools. Many coaches, principals, and directors of coaching programs use a brochure to describe the coach's roles to staff members.

For coaching programs to remain responsive to schools' and districts' current conditions and needs, decision makers should review and re-evaluate the coaches' roles annually. District and school conditions change over time, leading coaching roles to shift or expand.

As coaches become more experienced and develop their expertise through professional learning, they, too, can decide how to expand their roles. When coaching programs mature, teachers and coaches achieve their goals and are ready to set new ones.

Scenario

Franktown School District, a large urban district, had always operated very traditionally. When the district formed its coaching program, administrators did not consult the teachers association. Many teachers saw coaching as an administrative or supervisory position. As a result, most resisted coaching and collaboration, and the culture was, "We do not go into one another's classroom or hold ourselves responsible for other teachers' students."

When a new superintendent took charge, she began working with the teachers association to create a more productive coaching program. After considerable collaboration, the association leaders put their support behind the program and agreed that coaches would be hired based on knowledge and skills rather than seniority.

As the district hired new coaches, another issue became increasingly clear: The job description for the position was poorly defined. Without clear roles, many new coaches spent their first months doing whatever their building administrator or teachers asked.

Diego Alexander, one of the coaches, was frustrated and over-whelmed by multiple requests and expectations. He was uncertain to whom he was responsible and had no criteria to use to decide how to structure his daily work. He consulted with his fellow coaches in other schools and learned that some spent their day analyzing data for principals and creating useful charts and tables, while in other schools, the coaches conducted demonstration lessons for teachers. Teachers were asking coaches for services they heard another coach at another building was providing. Even the more experienced coaches were frustrated about what — and whose — direction to follow.

District leaders began to understand the need to define coaching roles to build some consistency into the program and help ensure coaches' success. First, both district and association leadership agreed that a teacher's decision to work with a coach would be voluntary and that all coaching interactions would be confidential.

They next identified four roles coaches would fill in the first year of the revised program:

- Data coach, because teachers had so much data and yet were not using the data to make instructional decisions;
- Instructional specialist, because changes in student achievement depend on changes in classroom instruction;
- Facilitator of learning so teachers gain the essential knowledge and skills needed to change classroom instruction; and
- Learner so the coach gains the essential knowledge and skills to be successful in the role.

Another change was to provide regular time for professional learning for all coaches. Coaches engaged in professional learning together every Friday, and at least once a month, principals joined them for a half day of shared learning.

After the district defined the coach's roles, Alexander and his principal created a brochure for the staff that described his services and how to access the coach. Alexander and his principal used the brochure to clarify for staff what services Alexander was able to provide.

Teachers referred to the brochure over the next months to clarify their understanding of Alexander's role and request appropriate services from him. Alexander began to feel he was getting requests for support that would have a more significant effect on his school's highly diverse and high-needs students. He began to feel more confident as a coach, although he knew he still had a lot to learn. By the end of his first year, Alexander and his principal began planning how to reintroduce his roles and responsibilities to staff at the beginning of the next year — and he planned to add the exciting role of catalyst for change to his responsibilities.

Reflection questions

- Engaging all stakeholder groups in early decisions about coaching became problematic for Franktown School District. What could be done to avoid similar challenges?

- What questions, issues, or challenges have arisen or are likely to emerge from various stakeholder groups? How will or have you responded to them?

- How might similar oversight affect your school or district? What have you done or might you do as a school or district to encourage widespread support for the coaching program?

- How are coaches' roles and responsibilities described? What changes would you make based on this chapter and the experiences of coaches in Franktown School District?

- Top district leaders are a significant factor in the coaching program's success. What lessons did you take away from the new superintendent in Franktown that you can use and share with your district's top leaders?

Recommendations for

Central office administrators

- Create a document that defines the roles for all personnel involved with the coaching program, from the superintendent to teachers.
- Identify roles for coaches annually, and describe the roles in writing to pass out to all staff.
- Set expectations for coaches' roles based on district and school improvement goals for student achievement.
- Focus coaches' work on strengthening the quality of teaching in all classrooms.
- Set the expectation for all teachers to work with coaches rather than just those who volunteer in order to expand coaching's impact.
- Create guidelines for how coaches allocate their time; for example: *Coaches spend 70% of their time working with teams of teachers or individual teachers in classrooms and spend a minimal amount of their time on administrative duties.*

Building administrators

- Communicate coaches' defined roles to all staff members.
- Establish a systematic process for determining whether a coach works with some or all of the teachers at a building.
- Create opportunities for teachers to choose how to work with the coach.
- Consider ways for coaches to build teachers' leadership capacity that will allow others to assume some coaching responsibilities, such as facilitating data conversations and conducting peer observations, so coaches can shift to more advanced responsibilities.
- Protect coaches' time so their work focuses on their defined roles.
- Talk frequently with the school's coach about how he or she is allocating time, and compare allocations to expectations.
- Identify barriers to meeting expectations, and implement strategies to overcome those barriers.

Coaches

- Create a written document for staff members that defines the coach's roles and how staff members can access coaching services.
- Focus on high-leverage services by helping teachers identify creative alternatives to get support for low-leverage services.
- When possible, work in teachers' classrooms.
- Assume all teachers want to improve and to work with a coach.
- Make coaching productive so teachers see immediate results for themselves and their students.
- Coach potential teacher leaders and make leadership skills, knowledge, and practices transparent to involve more teachers in leadership.
- Monitor time and adjust time allocation based on the district's expectations for defined roles.

TOOL INDEX
Chapter 5

	TOOL	PURPOSE
5.1	**Coaching roles**	Refer to this chart for a quick guide to a coach's roles.
5.2	**Framework for instructional coaching**	Get a description of all central office and building level personnel involved in this example of a coaching/teacher leader program.
5.3	**Coach time allocation**	Review how coaches spend time in various roles.
5.4	**Webber coaches**	Review one school's description of its coaches' roles, including the specific ways in which they work with various staff members.
5.5	**Roles of coaches**	Use this tool to make decisions about the level of priority for each of the coach's designated roles.

To download tools, see www.learningforward.org/publications/coachingmatters

Hiring
and placing coaches

O ne of the most important decisions districts or schools can make to ensure a quality coaching program is hiring the right people. The quality of the coach is directly related to how successful the coaching program is. Finding qualified candidates for the coach's position seems like an easy task. Principals or district leaders look first to highly successful teachers as potential candidates. They might look at other criteria, such as seniority, displacement, or surplus. No matter where the search begins, and whether the coaching program is brand new or a decade old, hiring and placement require thoughtful deliberation.

Sustaining a pool of viable coach candidates is increasingly important as the coaching program matures and coaches are hired into other leadership positions within the district. Coaches often become a pool from which future district and school administrators are selected because they are well prepared as instructional leaders. Given that the coaching

> A coach who is well suited for the job can make a significant difference — bringing about positive changes in teaching and learning.

program may be a stepping-off point for leadership succession, the process for hiring and placing coaches has even greater significance.

Hiring the best-qualified candidates for coaching positions in school districts involves school and district leaders making a series of decisions about coaches and the coaching program.

A coach who is well suited for the job can make a significant difference — bringing about positive changes in teaching and learning. Conversely, a coach who is poorly suited for the job might add to a culture of mistrust, denigrate professional development, and damage the integrity and credibility of coaching and coaches.

Ask these questions before hiring a coach

Hiring the best-qualified candidates for coaching positions in school districts involves school and district leaders making a series of decisions about coaches and the coaching program.

- What is the coach job description? What roles are coaches expected to serve? What are they required to know and be able to do to be successful?

- Who is responsible for hiring coaches?

- If the principals of the schools in which the coaches will work do not hire coaches or if coaches will work in multiple schools, who will decide the coaches' placements?

- What are the primary criteria for selecting coaches, and how will those criteria be used equitably across schools?

- How will those who hire coaches learn what coaches are expected to know and do in order to hire the best candidate?

- How will schools' unique characteristics or conditions be considered when hiring and placing coaches?

- Will the district prescreen candidates for coaching positions or create a pool of qualified candidates who are prepared to fill vacancies when they emerge?

- Will there be a limit on the tenure of a coach?

Use criteria to select coaches

School and district leaders need to be clear about what they want coaching to accomplish as they design the coaching program. That clarity should come through in the job descriptions.

For example, some districts want coaches to improve instruction in general. Others may want coaches to improve student learning in a specific content area, such as mathematics or literacy, and they will have to emphasize in the job description that candidates should have strong backgrounds in math or literacy content and instruction.

Those who will evaluate the coaching program should write the coach job description. If the program is designed at the district level and a central office administrator is overseeing it, district-level administrators should define the coach's roles and responsibilities to align with the district's vision. However, because principals are ultimately accountable for implementing district initiatives and will be working with the coaches to do so, it makes sense to involve principals in developing the job description. Leaders also may find it appropriate to involve teachers, current coaches, other resource personnel, and the teachers association to get ideas from all those impacted by coaching and to ensure that everyone is on board with the program.

The job description should clearly outline the coach's essential roles and responsibilities, along with the skills and qualifications candidates need to succeed in the role. When the job description is incomplete or vague, candidates are misled — or those making hiring decisions may select candidates who will not be able to meet the unstated expectations.

Joellen Killion and Cindy Harrison (2006) describe a set of attributes that are important for coaches to demonstrate in order to be able to influence significant school improvement. (See Chapter 3.) Candidates who are recognized and respected as colleagues, who engage in continuous improvement, who work well with others in collaborative ways, and who have the potential to develop their knowledge and skills as coaches are more likely to succeed in the role.

Create a hiring process

Defining a fair and thoughtful process for screening and interviewing potential candidates and then ranking them according to predetermined criteria generally results in more effective hiring decisions for any position. Because the coach often is responsible for demonstrating model lessons, an effective selection process might include planning and delivering a model lesson (Knight, 2004). A process that uses an application, portfolio, demonstration, and interviews ensures that candidates will be identified who are best suited for the position.

> Because the coach often is responsible for demonstrating model lessons, an effective selection process might include planning and delivering a model lesson.

Interviewers might include representatives of those who will be affected by the coaching. For example, if coaches are hired at the district level before being assigned to individual schools, the interview panel might include principals and teachers who will receive coaching services. Having multiple perspectives in the selection creates a richer decision-making process. Including teachers whom the coaches will serve increases teachers' feelings of responsibility for the program's success.

Districts and schools sometimes face difficult decisions that affect how they hire candidates. Hiring policies or agreements may limit the district's ability to open the position to all candidates. Teachers may need to be considered first if they have been surplused because of declining student enrollment or school closures; have priority in the hiring process because of their status, hiring date, or level of expertise; or have not yet been assigned to a school or classroom.

> Coach candidates must have the capacity to serve teachers as instructional leaders, grow professionally to learn how to coach, and have the flexibility and organizational skills to work in leadership roles.

Some schools or districts make the mistake of selecting a coach using criteria that are poorly aligned to the role expectations or selecting a coach without a fair and thoughtful screening and selection process. For example, a principal might be tempted to designate a support staff member already working in the school as coach, such as a special education teacher or a technology specialist. The principal might want to hire a special education teacher who is highly effective with children but who may not be suited to coach adults unless the program provides extensive professional development to prepare the teacher for this role change. The district may want to shift a literacy teacher whose role is being eliminated into the coaching role.

Coach candidates must have the capacity to serve teachers as instructional leaders, grow professionally to learn how to coach, and have the flexibility and organizational skills to work in leadership roles. Selecting coaches using seniority or longevity in the school as criteria — rather than a demonstration of viable characteristics listed in a thoughtful job description — is a mistake. Table 6.1 shows some of the characteristics principals have considered in hiring a coach. Circumstances do not always permit districts to use an ideal hiring process, but administrators should be vigilant about the selection processes to be certain that only those with the highest qualifications are selected as coaches.

Placing a competent person in the coaching role will affect the success of the coach and the coaching program, especially when the coaching program is new in the school or district. Hiring the right person creates the potential for accomplishing the student achievement goals for which schools and districts are being held accountable. Table 6.1 shows criteria principals report using when hiring a coach.

Placing coaches

Coaches are selected and placed based on the coaching program's purpose and the coach job description. If the program's goal is to support how a particular curricular program or district initiative is implemented, central administrators often select coaches and place them in schools using established criteria. In these cases, the principals in the receiving schools may need to be involved in deciding on placements in order to build their commitment to the coaching program and to the coach's success.

What coaches are expected to do in their role is another factor in placing coaches. If the job

Table 6.1 Percentage of principals who consider the following criteria "to a great extent" when hiring a reading coach for their schools

The coach's knowledge of reading instruction and best practices	91%
The coach's "people skills" and ability to work well with teachers	79%
The coach's classroom teaching experience	78%
The coach had or was working toward the reading endorsement	71%
The coach's oral presentation skills and ability to lead teacher groups and facilitate reflection	70%
The coach's experience working with students similar to our school's population	68%
The coach's experience working at the middle school level	62%
The coach's experience working with teachers to improve their practice	62%

Source: Marsh, J., McCombs, J., Lockwood, J.R., Martorell, F., Gershwin, D., et al. (2008). *Supporting literacy across the Sunshine State: A study of Florida middle school reading coaches.* Santa Monica, CA: RAND Corp.

description reflects the program's purpose and goals along with the coach's roles and responsibilities in achieving those goals, the job description is a useful tool in hiring and placement.

Another factor in considering a coach's placement is the school environment. District staff have planned to place a coach in a school with inadequate instructional leadership as a way to compensate for that lack. Coaches cannot substitute for school leaders. Asking coaches to serve as the school's instructional leader compromises the coach role and the role of the principal.

At other times, administrators who want improvement have decided to place coaches in all of the district's lowest-performing schools. Placement must take into consideration the school staff's readiness to have a coach and to benefit from coaching.

> Coaches cannot substitute for school leaders. Asking coaches to serve as the school's instructional leader compromises the coach role and the role of the principal.

Those deciding placement should ask:

- How does the school's principal demonstrate instructional leadership and convey a clear and articulated vision for effective teaching and student learning?
- What is the school culture?
- To what degree are teachers committed to continuous improvement, willing to collaborate, and eager to improve their practice and student results?

Coaches can spend an inordinate amount of time breaking down barriers to effective teaching in schools where staff are reluctant or unwilling to change; feel ambivalent, hopeless, or negative about students' capacity to learn; or single out students and families as responsible for poor student performance. Some schools simply aren't ready for coaching.

Coaches, regardless of their expertise, are not able to transform a school single-handedly. Conditions must be favorable to coaching, and coaches must have the support, skills, and

> However coaches are selected and placed, district staff and principals need explicit agreements about who supervises the coaches' work, who is responsible for supporting them, and how the principal and school district leaders will contribute to the coaches' and program's success.

resources to make a difference. Before sending a coach into any school, leaders should be willing to give the coach time to demonstrate that coaching can affect teaching quality and student learning.

Another factor in placing a coach is where the coach has worked. Placing a new coach in the school where the coach once taught has advantages and disadvantages. The coach has the advantage of knowing the staff, so building trust may be easier; however, creating a new identity as a coach rather than a fellow teacher may be difficult. Coaches will need opportunities to develop productive relationships with the teachers and the school leader. In schools where they have taught, it may be challenging for coaches to use coaching strategies with colleagues with whom they already have relationships. Table 6.2 summarizes the advantages and disadvantages of coach placement.

However coaches are selected and placed, district staff and principals need explicit agreements about who supervises the coaches' work, who is responsible for supporting them, and how the principal and school district leaders will contribute to the coaches' and program's success. Coaches, too, need a clear understanding of their work conditions, who their supervisor is, and who provides them with what type of support.

District leaders frequently supervise and support the coaches, particularly if coaches serve in more than one school. If coaching is aimed at improving student achievement within a particular school or a coach is working only in a single school, the principal may supervise the coach and share responsibility with district staff for providing support. If lines are not clear, coaches sometimes experience friction that can erode their clarity about their role.

Table 6.2 Considerations for placing a coach

PLACEMENT OF COACH	ADVANTAGES	DISADVANTAGES
In the school where the coach was a teacher	The coach: • Knows the staff and community. • Is familiar with student achievement data. • Has credibility teaching the students. • Has built trust with other teachers. • Knows the politics and interaction patterns of staff members. • Knows the unwritten rules for getting things done.	The coach: • May not be willing to push the district's agenda. • May be too close to particular people and so be perceived as part of the "in group." • May not ask the hard questions because he or she accepts the school as doing the best it can do. • May have a close relationship with the principal so confidentiality could be perceived as an issue.
In a school other than where the coach was a teacher	The coach: • Has fresh eyes to look at student achievement. • Has no previous friendships to pay attention to. • Is able to build relationships with all staff members equally. • Does not know the politics among staff so all get a fresh start.	The coach: • Needs time to build trust. • Needs time to figure out informal relationships and who influences whom. • May not have credibility with staff. • Has to get to know building data and the community.

Scenario

A large district faced a pressing need to improve student achievement and decided to invest in a coaching program districtwide. District leaders planned to add a half-time coach at each of the more than 120 schools.

District leaders wrote a job description based on coaching responsibilities defined by the funding sources and started to hire coaches immediately, as there were only eight weeks before school started. Over two months, the district hired more than 90 coaches and assigned them to schools. Although the principals were not involved in decisions about coach placement, they were happy to have additional instructional support and didn't complain.

In the program's first year, it became clear that some coaches were not right for the job and others' skills or personalities were not a good match for their schools. As more conflicts emerged, Jasperena Sanders, the central office coordinator in charge of the program, knew something had to change. She convened a committee with representatives from the teachers association, principals, classroom teachers, current successful coaches, and other central office personnel who had been involved in coaching, and asked them to rewrite the job description. Sanders was excited to see the team's enthusiasm as group members refined the process for hiring, selecting, and placing coaches.

In early spring of that first year, the coaches were notified that they would need to reapply for the newly reconfigured positions. The positions were opened to other candidates as well. Some coaches were ready to return to their prior positions or wanted to apply for jobs other than coach. About 70% of the coaches reapplied for coaching positions.

Later in the spring, Sanders formed a different committee to screen candidates and determine which would be included in a candidate pool. The district intentionally placed more candidates in the pool than there were current positions in order to have people available for the inevitable situations in which a coach was needed after the school year began.

Next, each school formed its own selection committee. Committee members reviewed the credentials of the candidates in the pool they wanted to consider for their school, interviewed them, and made a recommendation to the school's principal, who made the final decision about which coach to bring to the school.

With the new process, 95% of the coach placements seemed successful, and the coaches' effectiveness was evident in teacher and principal satisfaction with coaching, improvements in school culture, and improved student achievement in 92% of the district's buildings.

Each year after that, Sanders evaluated the hiring and placement process and made small adjustments as necessary. Overall evaluations of the coaching program continued to improve each year, and support for coaching and individual coaches continued to grow. Sanders also found that the pool of coach candidates continued to improve and that the district continued to have an ample supply of carefully selected candidates ready to be placed as coaches.

Reflection questions

- What might have contributed to the problems coaches experienced in the first year of this new coaching program?

- What effect did Sanders involving a number of people in revamping the coaching role and the hiring and placement process have on rehiring and coach placement? Explain.

- How are coaches in your district hired and placed? What effect did the process have on the coaches' and the program's success? Why did the district select its process?

- Some districts use a central office-driven process similar to Sanders' district. What are the advantages and disadvantages of hiring and placing coaches through the central office rather than using a school-based process?

- What steps did Sanders use in the hiring and placement process, and how would you modify them?

Recommendations for

Central office administrators

- Be certain the coach job description explicitly explains coaches' roles and responsibilities.
- Select coaches based on the expectations outlined in the job description.
- Establish a task force of representatives from all stakeholder groups to collaborate in designing the coach selection process.
- Establish clear criteria for selecting coaches.
- Be clear about any parameters for applying for the coach position.
- Be clear about who makes the final decision in hiring coaches.
- Provide an explicit, transparent process for hiring coaches.
- Provide opportunities for potential candidates to ask questions about the role, particularly if the role is new to the district or school.
- Provide opportunities for potential candidate to interact with existing coaches to ask questions and to learn more about the role.

Building administrators

- Be clear about the coaches' roles and responsibilities.
- Maintain a transparent hiring process for coaches that aligns with federal, state, and district hiring guidelines.
- Understand the district staff's role in selecting school-based coaches.
- Make the decision-making process explicit.
- Engage stakeholders in the hiring process.
- Select a coach based on the individual's capacity to meet the expectations of the role as defined in the job description.
- Provide opportunities for potential candidates to ask questions about the role, particularly if the role is new to the district or school.
- Provide opportunities for potential candidates to interact with existing coaches to ask questions and to learn more about the role.

Coaches

- Offer input on the coach's job description to update it for the hiring process.
- Provide input on coaches' roles and responsibilities in order to inform potential candidates.
- Interact with potential candidates to help them understand coaches' roles and responsibilities.
- Share information about the application process with potential candidates.
- Maintain neutrality in all aspects of the hiring process.
- Maintain confidentiality about the hiring process.

TOOL INDEX
Chapter 6

	TOOL	PURPOSE
6.1	**Teacher on special assignment/ elementary instructional coach job description**	Use this sample job description as a guide when advertising for an elementary instructional coach.
6.2	**High school language arts instructional coach job description and responsibilities**	Examine the responsibilities of a high school language arts instructional coach based on this district's example.
6.3	**Instructional coach job description**	Consider using Michigan's job description for instructional coaches hired through a Title I accountability grant as a guide for your own job description.
6.4	**GEAR UP coach planning template**	Study this template in which GEAR UP coaches describe their roles.
6.5	**Elementary school instructional coach interview questions**	Use these sample questions and indicators of potential when interviewing elementary school instructional coach candidates.
6.6	**Middle school instructional coach interview questions**	Use these sample questions and indicators of potential when interviewing middle school instructional coach candidates.
6.7	**Middle school instructional coach written interview questions**	Use this sample questionnaire to obtain a writing sample from coach candidates.
6.8	**Proposed process for coach placement**	Take steps to place coach candidates in school positions.

To download tools, see www.learningforward.org/publications/coachingmatters

Professional learning
for coaches

Acoaching program's success depends on the quality of the coaching, and the quality of the coaching depends on the quality of preparation and support those selected to be coaches receive. Successful coaching requires understanding specific content related to the role. Effective coaching programs help coaches gain that understanding by providing differentiated professional support for coaches throughout their careers. Good coaching programs begin with some degree of professional development up front, before or soon after the coach takes the position.

As part of their role, coaches commit to acquiring and strengthening the knowledge, skills, attitudes, and beliefs they need in order to carry out their responsibilities. Their success is closely linked to ongoing learning and support to use their learning in their work.

When coaches try to serve teachers without having developed some basic skills and attitudes toward their role, they may make mistakes that are difficult to overcome. When a teacher's initial experience with the coach is less than satisfactory, the coach will have a hard time getting a second opportunity with that teacher.

Good coaching programs offer ongoing professional learning throughout each year of implementation to ensure that coaches have up-to-date knowledge and the skills to lead professional learning in their schools.

Coaches need layers of learning

Coaches are most likely to succeed when schools and districts provide them with research- and standards-based professional development aligned to their job description and the district's curriculum. Professional development that builds coaches' capacity is designed and implemented in accordance with Learning Forward's *Standards for Professional Learning*. (See box on p. 87.)

Good coaching programs offer ongoing professional development to ensure that coaches have up-to-date knowledge and the skills to lead professional learning in their schools.

Successful districts tap experienced and skilled facilitators to ensure that coaches, who are so instrumental to improvement efforts, receive the best possible professional development to foster their motivation and enthusiasm for learning. Those who design and facilitate coaches' learning experiences and also model effective professional learning allow coaches to understand professional learning on two levels: how it affects their own learning and how to plan effective learning for others.

Coaching programs often focus on developing coaches' knowledge and skills only related to what teachers need to know and do and do not focus enough on how coaches work best with adult learners. Coaches first need to learn how to work effectively with adults. They need to know how adults learn, how to motivate and engage adults in learning, and how to help adults implement new practices in their classrooms.

One of the first things coaches need to understand is the human reaction to change. Districts often assume that coaches are masterful teachers who can quickly learn and implement new instructional practices and content. Most coaches are able to adapt and change — hallmarks of successful professionals and likely a factor in their selection as coaches. These districts often hire coaches to support innovations, yet they don't recognize the need to step up coaches' professional learning to help them facilitate change among their peers.

Change elicits a range of responses from people. The Concerns-Based Adoption Model, a body of research about change in education, offers practical lessons about those involved in change and guides coaches in how to facilitate change (Hall & Hord, 2010). Others who address change and people's experience with it, such as William Bridges, a career and life coach, provide insights that can guide coaches to respond effectively to teachers as they refine their practice.

Change is a developmental process

Gene Hall and Shirley Hord (2010) found that while people respond to change differently, some patterns occur in the developmental process. They describe this as Stages of Concern (see Table 7.1). The seven stages describe different types of concerns, feelings, or responses that people typically experience as they move from being unaware of the change to implementing and refining their use of the innovation. The example here uses concerns about implementing the Common Core State Standards.

Not everyone will move through all stages, nor will each person move at the same rate through the stages. Some may revisit a stage as they learn more about the innovation and learn new practices associated with it. For example, teachers implementing the math standards may experience the personal and management stages several times as they learn to modify their curriculum and as they learn new instructional practices. Each modification may result in repeating concerns.

Thomas Guskey and Dennis Sparks (1996) found that teachers developed positive attitudes about innovations after experiencing some success with the innovations. In other words, success breeds success. This research reminds coaches that success fosters greater willingness to implement the innovation. When teachers have evidence that the changes they are making in content and instruction are producing results in student achievement, they are more willing to continue to use the practices.

Change is personal

Individuals experience change differently. Some embrace change, while others resist it. Coaches must be ready to understand how individuals experience change, understand that each person's experience is valid, and respond to the individual's concerns and needs. By listening to teachers' comments and using the Stages of Concern (Table 7.1), coaches can identify pressing concerns and work with individuals or teams to address those concerns. A coach who recognizes concerns and responds can help alleviate potential challenges. When a coach ignores an expressed concern, the individual gets the message that his or her concerns are unimportant or inappropriate and may resist the change.

In the following example, the responses show how a coach acknowledges the personal nature of change. This difference is defined in Table 7.2. Readers may want to think about how they would respond to the teacher.

Teacher: I've worked hard for years to refine my instructional units to be sure my students are ready for the end-of-year assessments. My students have done well on the assessments in the last three years, and I'm proud of that. Now, here comes a new curriculum. I don't know how I'm going to give up everything I've done and start all over. It doesn't seem fair to my students or to me.

Coach response 1: All teachers are required to implement the new curriculum and assessments. I look forward to helping you with the changes. When we meet as a team next week, we'll discuss how to design new units that integrate the new curriculum.

Coach response 2: It's clear that you carefully and thoughtfully planned the entire year's curriculum so that students are ready for the state assessment, and that your efforts have paid off. It's also easy to understand why you feel that your students' success resulting from your hard work is not fairly recognized. I want to hear more about what you anticipate the new curriculum will mean in terms of your work. What do you worry about the most? What are some ways I can support you as you begin to make the changes you want to make?

Coaches acknowledge the personal nature of change by shifting their interactions with teachers.

Change occurs over time

Change is not a light-switch action. It requires time, ongoing learning, trial and error, continuous refinement, and substantial support. By recognizing where individual teachers are along a continuum in

Table 7.1 Stages of concern about Common Core State Standards*

	STAGES OF CONCERN	RESPONSE FROM A TEACHER ABOUT COMMON CORE STATE STANDARDS	POSSIBLE COACH RESPONSE
Impact	**6** Refocus	I have been adapting the curricula to meet the needs of English language learners in my classroom. I want to expand the use of these strategies in my class and encourage others to use them.	I'd like to learn about the adaptations and refinements you are making, what prompted the need for them, and how you are assessing the effects of these adaptations on your teaching and student learning.
	5 Collaboration	I am looking forward to working with other teachers to revise our classroom curricula, formative assessments, and instructional strategies.	Which colleagues have you been working with as you implement the curricula? How is this collaboration contributing to your work? What do you want to learn in your collaboration with colleagues?
Task	**4** Consequence	I hope the new standards and curricula will help all my students be ready for college and careers. I worry about my English language learner students and how those with special needs will respond to the new standards and curricula.	Describe how you will know if the new standards affect student learning. What indicators of student success will you see in your classroom as you interact with students? How well do those indicators apply to English language learners and students with special needs?
	3 Management	We are doing so many other new initiatives. How will we be able to implement a completely new set of standards and curricula at the same time? I wonder how we will have the time and resources to make the changes the new curricula require.	Let's think about multiple ways we can manage the demands of the new standards and curricula. I wonder what is already is in place to help you. Let's concentrate our efforts on those areas where we have fewer resources as a starting point.

Table 7.1 Stages of concern about Common Core State Standards* (cont'd)

	STAGES OF CONCERN	RESPONSE FROM A TEACHER ABOUT COMMON CORE STATE STANDARDS	POSSIBLE COACH RESPONSE
Self	**2** Personal	I am not sure how the Common Core State Standards will affect my teaching.	What are some ways you expect the standards will influence your teaching? What worries you? What excites you?
	1 Information	Many people seem to be talking about the standards and I want to know more.	What do you know already about the Common Core standards? I can connect you with other teachers who are beginning to implement the standards if you want to learn about their work.
	0 Awareness	We won't implement the new standards for another year, so I can't worry about them now.	Yes, we have another year before full implementation, and I know you are focusing your energy on your students' success this year. I have some information that other teachers are compiling about how their teaching is changing if you are interested in having it.

* Note: The Stages of Concern begin with 0 and move through 6.

Source: Hall, G. & Hord, S. (2010). *Implementing change: Patterns, principles, and potholes.* Upper Saddle River, NJ: Pearson.

using the innovation, coaches can tailor their support to help individuals move up the levels of use.

The levels of use, illustrated in Table 7.3 on p. 82, is a framework coaches can use to determine to what extent a teacher is implementing a new practice so the coach can plan how best to support the teacher. As coaches interact with teachers in individual or team planning and in reflective conversations about their practices, they can focus on the journey toward full implementation; providing constructive feedback and opportunities for teachers to learn the knowledge, skills, and practices they need to achieve the next level; recognizing successful practice; and providing differentiated support. When coaches remind teachers that change is a process, teachers gain confidence because they recognize that adapting their instruction to implement the new standards is not always easy or fast.

Coaches remain flexible and fluid in their interactions with teachers rather than trying to "fix" teachers who have particular concerns or level of use, because both the level of use and the stage of concern a teacher acknowledges can shift

Table 7.2 Coaches' interaction changes

FROM	TO
Directing	Inquiring
Correcting	Providing constructive feedback
Accepting	Empowering
Focusing on strategies	Focusing on beliefs
Making excuses	Generating possibilities
Advising	Listening

with context, with familiarity with the content or pedagogy, and how students are learning.

Mindsets matter

How people think about change influences how they approach it. This is true for coaches and teachers. A coach's mindset influences the coach's ability to support teachers. Coaches with a mindset of appreciation, inquiry, and assets will have safe and constructive relationships with their colleagues. When a coach's mindset is limited by judgment and focused on the gap between the ideal and current practice, the coach will have a more difficult time acknowledging teachers' small successes, may not value progress over time, and may not have the patience and perseverance to help teachers become independent with the new practices. These coaches may be more directive, neglect to listen to individual needs or concerns, and fail to provide appropriate support.

The following examples of coach-teacher interactions demonstrate an appreciative, inquiry, and asset approach and a deficit focus. Readers will want to think about how they would feel as the teacher in each situation.

Teacher: This new curriculum is making me crazy. We spend way too much time on the same thing. Asking students to explain their

thinking for every problem doesn't tell me if they can solve the problem. Isn't that what's important in math?

Coach response 1: The new math standards call for changes in math curriculum and instruction. While it's important for students to solve problems and get answers they can defend, the curriculum makes it clear that it is more important that students are able to determine one or more ways to approach a problem, have a sense of the kind of math required in it, and can explain their problem solving. The curriculum asks for this deeper kind of thinking from students, not just answers.

Coach response 2: The new curriculum is causing us to think differently about math. I appreciate what you are saying about feeling that you are spending too much time on the same thing. I want to understand more about what you are saying first. I heard you mention two ideas. One is that you spend too much time on one topic, and the second is that having students explain their thinking doesn't give you the information you want about whether they understand math well enough to solve the problems. Let's talk about these ideas. Where shall we start?

A coach who recognizes and appreciates the struggle of change is more likely to convey a message that dissonance is a natural and necessary part of the change process and that persistence and effort will pay off. A coach's curiosity and inquiry foster curiosity and inquiry in teachers, helping them maintain a healthy mindset that leads to continuous improvement.

Coaches have four areas of expertise

To focus on what teachers need to know and effectively help teachers grow, coaches also need to understand that knowing the content area, knowing how to teach, knowing how to teach the content area, and knowing how students learn the content are distinct areas of expertise.

Lee Shulman (1998) describes these four types of knowledge that effective teachers need:

- Content knowledge;
- General knowledge about instructional practices;
- Knowledge about how students learn; and
- Knowledge about how students learn a specific discipline, which Shulman terms pedagogical content knowledge.

In addition, coaches need to understand how adults learn. As coaches become more experienced, their professional development shifts from building the knowledge and skills they need to work with adult learners to developing expertise. Coaches who add that important layer of content knowledge increase the effectiveness of their work. They also must be able to explain clearly the most effective strategies in their own practices to demonstrate expertise.

Coaches who focus on specific subjects should receive additional professional development in that discipline. For example, literacy coaches are more credible to teachers when they demonstrate that they have background knowledge in literacy, as well as the skills to plan and deliver an effective literacy lesson. Coaches who are focusing on improving mathematic or science instruction are more influential if they have expertise in those content areas.

Coaches who are generalists or instructional coaches work with teachers to improve instructional practices rather than focusing on a specific subject area. Instructional coaches are most effec-

As coaches become more experienced, their professional development shifts from building the knowledge and skills they need to work with adult learners to developing expertise.

tive when they demonstrate expertise not only in the academic content and student content standards, but also in how students learn.

In their early work with coaches, mentor coaches or supervisors who differentiate their support to novice coaches help them become comfortable with the role more quickly. They offer focused and constructive feedback and help new coaches reflect regularly on the effect of their work, using data to make ongoing adjustments.

Coaches also need opportunities to be active members of their own collaborative learning teams in which they learn with and from one another, seek and receive support, and engage in inquiry through action research. They may develop annual portfolios of artifacts related to this professional learning.

Some districts have developed an advisory group — of coach champions, individual coaches, representatives of the primary client group, principals, and central office staff — who can offer input to those responsible for coaches' professional development. The advisory group uses data about student learning, teacher performance, coach performance,

Table 7.3 Levels of use of Common Core State Standards

	LEVEL OF USE	DESCRIPTION	POSSIBLE COACH RESPONSE
Advanced use	**Renewal**	The teacher is seeking ways to improve results for all students, perhaps through using different instructional practices such as flexible grouping or other alternatives that will strengthen implementation with fidelity of Common Core State Standards and will improve student achievement.	Tell me about refinements you are making because you weren't seeing the results you had hoped to see. How are those changes you are making affecting student learning? How can we help others learn about and implement these refinements?
	Integration	The teacher is coordinating use of the Common Core standards with others, such as working collaboratively with peers in learning communities, working with a coach, and meeting with colleagues in local or global communities of practice.	What professional learning goals are you and your collaborative learning team working on now, and how are you structuring your learning? How is collaboration with your colleagues helping you minimize variance in student learning across classrooms and schools? What benefits are you realizing from collaboration? What are the challenges to collaboration and how are you addressing them?
	Refinement	The teacher is seeking to improve practice, gathering input, and making changes to improve student results.	Tell me about the kinds of feedback that will be most helpful to you as you implement the standards. How best can I provide you with constructive feedback? What types of data do you want me to help you gather and analyze as you refine your practice?

Table 7.3 Levels of use of Common Core State Standards (cont'd)

	LEVEL OF USE	DESCRIPTION	POSSIBLE COACH RESPONSE
Early stage	**Routine**	The teacher is using the standards with some regularity, yet seeking no or very limited feedback on how to improve practice, and making minimal changes based on the feedback.	Tell me about how you use the standards to plan instruction, reflect on your work, and assess student performance. Which standards make most sense to you as you use them? Which standards seem more challenging to implement? How do you think your use of the standards is affecting your teaching and student learning?
	Mechanical	The teacher is using the standards, yet making decisions through his or her interpretation or perceptions of what is appropriate.	Let's look at several unit plans to develop _____ (a specific standard). How are they different? What are the strengths in each lesson? Which is most like how you teach the standard now? What are you observing in the other unit that might give you some ideas for your unit?

Source: Hall, G. & Hord, S. (2010). *Implementing change: Patterns, principles, and potholes* (3rd ed.). Upper Saddle River, NJ: Prentice Hall.

and school and district goals to provide input on coaches' professional development. Data-based guidance rather than wish-based guidance strengthens the link between what coaches know and do and the goals they are striving to achieve.

Well-designed professional development for coaches also includes an opportunity for the coaches to evaluate their own professional development at the end of each session. Coaches' satisfaction is one indicator of whether the professional development is effective. In addition to satisfaction surveys, other indicators are surveys of principals and teachers asking the extent to which they believe coaches' support is better enabling them to carry out their responsibilities, and data about the structures and processes in

place in the school or district to support coaching. Asking teachers about how coaches have supported them in specific areas and observing teachers in their classrooms to see the extent to which they are implementing practices they have learned from the coaches are additional measures for assessing the professional development's relevancy and effectiveness. Correlating coach professional development and improved instruction and student performance is a valuable goal. (See Chapter 11 on evaluation.)

Build learning into the design

Coaches value the opportunity for structured support and to learn with and from each other. Coaching programs can address coaches' ongoing

Principles of adult learning

1. **Needs assessment.** Learners participate in naming what is to be learned.

2. **Safety.** Individuals are secure in the environment and the process.

3. **Relationship.** The learning facilitator and the learner have a sound relationship for learning and development.

4. **Sequence and reinforcement.** The learning facilitator pays careful attention to the sequence of content and reinforcement for transfer of the content into routine practice.

5. **Praxis.** The learner acts and then reflects on the action and its results in a learning-by-doing process.

6. **Respect.** The learning facilitator acknowledges that adults are decision makers and demonstrates respect for adult learners as they study the content and themselves in the learning process.

7. **Cognitive, affective, and psychomotor aspects.** Learning is more than a cognitive process. Learning facilitators acknowledge and integrate learners' feelings and actions into the learning process.

8. **Immediacy.** The learning is relevant to imminent needs.

9. **Roles.** Teachers and learners have clear roles in the learning process, preferably ones that promote dialogue and constructive exchanges of ideas.

10. **Teamwork.** Learners work in small groups.

11. **Engagement.** Learners are actively involved in what they are learning.

12. **Accountability.** Learners and teachers understand how learners know they know.

Source: Vella, J. (2002). *Learning to listen, learning to teach: The power of dialogue in educating adults.* San Francisco: Jossey-Bass.

needs by providing regular professional learning after the front-loaded professional development coaches get before beginning their work.

Coaches feel more supported and are more successful in their work when they have time for learning. Some school districts designate one full day a

Program designers can help smooth the way for coaches' professional learning by building it into the design.

week for coaches to get together to learn about best coaching practices and get updates on district initiatives. The professional learning also focuses on what coaches say they need, based on survey results. In addition, principals and teachers may provide input into what they believe their school needs, which affects what coaches need to know. Mentors and novice coaches can discuss how to apply the learning in their own contexts. (See Chapter 8 on support for the coaching program.)

Other school districts have half-day meetings each week, while still others bring coaches together once or twice a month. The most valuable part of regular meetings is the chance for coaches to discuss successes and challenges they face and to learn from one another.

Program designers can help smooth the way for coaches' professional learning by building it into the design and making the expectation clear at the program's outset. By communicating early on to teachers and principals what the coaches' calendar is and the rationale for coach professional learning, program leaders can avoid the opposition that sometimes develops to pulling coaches from their buildings to attend professional development.

One school district designing a coaching program formed a steering committee comprising staff developers, principals, teachers (potential coaches), union representatives, and executive-level leaders. The steering committee created a calendar with intensive, front-loaded professional development and ongoing professional learning. The committee continued to meet periodically during the program's initial stages to address potential concerns about the program's implementation; the committee also proactively communicated the intent and purpose behind coaches being out of the building regularly. By setting aside time in the calendar and letting all those affected know in advance, this district avoided complaints.

Coaching labs aid learning

One model for professional learning during coaches' regular meetings is a coaching laboratory, or coaching lab. In a coaching lab, a coach and teacher have a coaching session in a fishbowl setting — the coach engages the teacher in a conversation about a topic relevant to the teacher's instruction. As in any coaching session, the coach maintains consistency and consciousness about the strategies being used to facilitate the teacher's learning. Other coaches silently observe the conversation and take notes. When the coaching conversation is over, a skilled facilitator helps the group debrief. The facilitator encourages participants and observers to analyze different aspects of the coaching event for how they affect the coach and teacher. The facilitator asks the observers for specific examples of the coach's behaviors and language in the interaction, and how the coach's behaviors and language affected the teacher. Coaches can use what they learn to refine their skills and increase their repertoire of effective strategies for working with teachers.

Principals, coaches need joint learning

A final consideration for coaches' professional learning is the importance of having principals and coaches learn together in some instances. While principals do not need professional development in all of the same areas as coaches, they do need a clear understanding of the coach's work. When the principal's expectations and understanding of the coach's roles and responsibilities align with the coach's and the program designers', principals are better able to help the coach with day-to-day challenges, to help assess schoolwide needs and prioritize the coach's work, and to provide continual support.

When coaches are expected to help teachers implement district initiatives, having the coach and principal receive the same information at the same time about the initiative and having them in the same professional development is beneficial.

Principals also gain from having the chance to learn about coaches' work in other schools and can compare and consider how coaching can be improved in their own buildings.

Outcomes for coach learning

A well-designed coaching program offers coaches basic professional learning geared toward coaches having:

- Knowledge and understanding of various models of change and career development and how these models apply to adult learners.

- Understanding of the reasons that teachers may resist coaching and possible interventions to address resistive behavior.

- Knowledge of research-based instructional practices and of the skills needed to model such practices in teachers' classrooms, as well as to co-plan and co-teach.

- Effective interpersonal and communication skills for developing trusting, collaborative relationships with colleagues.

- The ability to assess student learning needs and to implement interventions with students who have widely different needs.

- The understanding of and ability to implement a learning cycle for a teacher, including planning, observing, collecting data, and reflecting with a client about the event.

- Effective facilitation skills for working with groups.

- Ability to design and deliver effective presentations.

- Understanding of what constitutes effective professional learning and how it relates to adult learning, as well as familiarity with a variety of professional development designs.

- Skills to help groups and individuals use data to make decisions about classroom instructional practices.

- Knowledge about teacher performance standards.

- Knowledge about the curriculum expectations for students.

Learning Forward's *Standards for Professional Learning*

Learning Communities: Professional learning that increases educator effectiveness and results for all students occurs within learning communities committed to continuous improvement, collective responsibility, and goal alignment.

Leadership: Professional learning that increases educator effectiveness and results for all students requires skillful leaders who develop capacity, advocate, and create support systems for professional learning.

Resources: Professional learning that increases educator effectiveness and results for all students requires prioritizing, monitoring, and coordinating resources for educator learning.

Data: Professional learning that increases educator effectiveness and results for all students uses a variety of sources and types of student, educator, and system data to plan, assess, and evaluate professional learning.

Learning Designs: Professional learning that increases educator effectiveness and results for all students integrates theories, research, and models of human learning to achieve its intended outcomes.

Implementation: Professional learning that increases educator effectiveness and results for all students applies research on change and sustains support for implementation of professional learning for long-term change.

Outcomes: Professional learning that increases educator effectiveness and results for all students aligns its outcomes with educator performance and student curriculum standards.

Source: www.learningforward.org.

Samantha Petersen was about to begin her first year as an instructional coach at Parkview Elementary School, where she had taught for the past five years. Although she was optimistic that, in time, she would feel more comfortable as a coach, Petersen lacked confidence about how she would carry out her new role, especially because her school had never had a coach and she had no model of coaching to learn from.

Petersen felt fortunate that her district supported its coaches in gaining needed skills and knowledge by offering two full days of professional development before the school year began, with regular follow-up sessions throughout the year. In the two days of sessions, she learned more about the scope of her responsibilities and considered how she would carry out her new position. Various exercises helped her learn how the coach's different roles can affect teachers' work. She appreciated having time during those two days to talk to coaches from other schools to compare ideas and consider alternatives.

The sessions also helped Petersen learn about the change process. As a teacher who had experienced many initiatives throughout her own career, she could relate to what the trainers said. She began to realize that her new role as a coach was a big change not only for her, but for all the teachers at her school. Although she knew her principal and colleagues perceived her as an effective classroom teacher and she had good relationships with most on the staff, the change in position meant she would need to re-form her relationships as staff came to recognize her coaching role.

District leaders also reviewed with the coaches how better to work with teachers who might resist change and offered strategies that, at least in theory, would help to bring those people along.

Scenario

The session leaders encouraged coaches to begin the year by scheduling time to meet with their principals to establish a partnership agreement that discussed specifically the principal's expectations for the coach role and to agree on how the coach would allocate coaching time. They asked coaches to reflect and make notes about their conversations.

The trainers next encouraged the coaches to try to apply immediately some of the things they learned about the change process and write brief reflective notes about what they observed about someone related to the change process. The trainers pledged time in the next coach professional development day for the coaches to meet in small groups to compare their experiences with the partnership agreement conversation and applying the change process.

Petersen looked forward to the next time she would be together with other coaches for professional learning. In the meantime, she also looked forward to working with her mentor, Julie Medina. Medina had offered to come to Parkview once each week in the beginning of the year to help Petersen get under way and help her think through some of her ideas. Petersen appreciated that she could confide in Medina about issues she was not comfortable sharing with anyone else. She and Medina established agreements about keeping their conversations confidential. Petersen also knew that if she had an urgent matter to talk over before Medina was scheduled to come to Parkview, she could call, email, or text Medina.

As a new instructional coach, Petersen was getting the support she needed to help fulfill the potential of the coach's role — to support teacher learning that would lead to greater student achievement — and she felt highly motivated as an educator to continue her own learning.

Reflection questions

- What did Petersen's district do to support her as a new coach? How does that support compare with coach support in your district or school?

- Why did Petersen lack confidence in her new role? To what degree do you think she was accurate in her feelings? Explain.

- Was the transition from classroom teacher to coach easy or difficult for the coaches you know? Describe your own or another coach's transition, and discuss what factors affected how the transition went.

- How do you feel about content on the change process being a part of coaches' early preparation? Explain.

- How likely is it for coaches to face resistance? How is resistance manifested? What are some of the most effective strategies for handling resistance?

Central office administrators

- Ensure that coaches' professional development aligns with their job description.
- Before launching a coaching program, plan and design intensive, front-loaded professional development for coaches.
- Include days in the school or district calendar for instructional coaches to participate in ongoing professional learning.
- Create a structure to ensure that coaches and principals offer input about how coaches' professional development is designed and delivered.
- Balance the content of the ongoing professional development between coaches' expressed needs and the district's needs to have coaches provide support for specific initiatives.
- Establish the expectations that principals and coaches attend professional development together when the learning pertains to district initiatives for which the coaches are expected to provide support.
- Designate mentors for novice coaches, and clearly define the roles of both the mentor and the protégé.

Building administrators

- Work with the coach to communicate to teachers that coaches need to attend professional development, even if doing so means the coach may be out of the building.
- Meet regularly with the coach to ask what professional support the coach needs.
- Sanction time for the coach to meet with his or her mentor during work time (as applicable).
- Attend professional development with the coach when appropriate.

Coaches

- Attend all professional development offered to support the work defined by your job description.
- Apply the learning from the professional development to the work in your own school.
- Provide honest feedback to the trainers regarding the extent to which your needs are met in professional development. Identify and voice your needs for further professional learning.

Recommendations for

TOOL INDEX
Chapter 7

	TOOL	PURPOSE
7.1	**Instructional coaches' program training**	Review topics and content outcomes for basic coach professional learning.
7.2	**Instructional coaches' ongoing Friday training: Facilitator's agenda**	Use this sample facilitator's agenda for a half-day professional learning session as a model for engaging coaches in learning.
7.3	**Instructional coaches' ongoing Friday training: Participants' agenda**	Use this sample participants' agenda for a half-day professional learning session as a model for engaging coaches in learning.
7.4	**Student achievement coach Friday training schedules**	Consider this sample yearlong professional development schedule for coaches in building your own.
7.5	**Coaches' professional development evaluation**	Create your own evaluation using sample questions for evaluating a professional learning session.
7.6	**Instructional coach feedback template: Conversation with the principal**	Have a coach-and-principal conversation to elicit feedback around these sample questions.
7.7	**Instructional coach feedback template: Conversation with teacher team members**	Use these sample questions to elicit feedback in conversation with teachers.
7.8	**Sample agenda for school-based coaches preparation training**	Determine your own topics after reviewing this outline of eight days of professional learning for coaches.
7.9	**Learning Forward Coaches Academy agenda**	Base your professional development on a typical one-day agenda from the Learning Forward Coaches Academy.
7.10	**Coaching lab prebrief**	Describes the process leading up to a coaching lab observation
7.11	**Learning lab debrief**	Review a process for debriefing the coaching lab observation.

To download tools, see www.learningforward.org/publications/coachingmatters

Support
for the coaching program

The goal of coaching programs is to increase student achievement by creating systemic change in the quality of teacher instruction. For coaching to be a powerful, systemic professional development intervention, however, coaches need support at every level. Coaches require:

* District support;

* Peer support;

* Principal support; and

* External support.

When all of these levels combine to support coaches in their role, the coaching program is more likely to be effective.

District support

District support provides coaches with the preparation, ongoing professional learning, and continuous support to succeed in their role. Coaches also gain a clear direction by aligning their work to the district's strategic plan, vision, and goals.

Coaches may get district-level support from a designated coach champion, who is a district-level administrator who has a vision for the coaching program and takes responsibility for overseeing the program. A champion — the program's advocate or defender — may be a district curriculum leader, federal program director, director of special projects, an assistant superintendent, or someone who fills several of these roles simultaneously.

Although district-level champions sometimes also serve in an evaluative role, the champion's primary role is to support and work with coaches. Champions often facilitate conferences between the principal and the coach several times each school year to discuss the program's integrity, successes, challenges, and opportunities for improvement; the coach's work; and

Coaches may get district-level support from a designated coach champion, who is a district-level administrator who has a vision for the coaching program and takes responsibility for overseeing the program.

professional learning the coach may need. These meetings ensure ongoing communication and maintain a focus on work expectations and program goals.

The coach's conversations with the champion and the principal allow the coach to offer insights into barriers and suggest needed resources. While most principals and coaches collaborate more frequently, these meetings give the coach an opportunity to stress accomplishments tied to school and district goals and relate coaching to school and district goals for student academic success.

The coach champion ideally takes the lead in training coaches. The champion meets regularly with other coordinators or evaluators and principals, and, when coaching issues arise at a specific building, helps solve problems and conflicts. For example, when a school or district administrator asks the coach to take on responsibilities outside of the coach's job description, such as working with small groups of students or reorganizing the book room, the coach champion may help the coach work with the principal to accomplish the work in a different way while protecting the coach's time to work with individual or teams of teachers. Coach champions also often help coaches address teacher resistance to coaching.

Effective champions visit schools often. The frequency of the visits depends on the number of coaches and schools a champion serves. While the ratio of coaches to coach champions varies, districts should be able to allow coach champions to visit coaches at least monthly, particularly when the program is new or coaches are novices. A 1:25 ratio of coach champions to coaches allows for monthly visits.

When the champion meets regularly with the coach and principal, the champion is able to support the coach and understand each coach's context. An added benefit is that the coaching champion who meets with many coaches can connect two coaches and schools to learn from one another, share resources, or spread effective practices across schools.

Peer support

Peer support helps coaches improve their ability to solve problems and practice their coaching skills. Coaches benefit from having a role-alike learning community for continuous professional learning and opportunities to collaborate with other coaches. They value other coaches' support to develop the knowledge, skills, dispositions, and practices of coaching. Because many work in isolation as the only coach in their school, having a trusted peer or a community of practice to turn to in order to solve problems and collaborate allows coaches to practice being reflective. With the peer support, coaches address problems of practice from diverse perspectives.

Districts may have several ways of offering coach-to-coach support. They may establish an induction program for novice coaches that includes an orientation and training. Some districts offer mentoring programs in which experienced coaches mentor novices. Buddy systems not based on experience levels give coaches opportunities for reciprocal, peer-to-peer support and strengthen collegiality. In other districts, coaches participate in communities of practice with other coaches.

Coaches, like all educators, must continually improve their practice to better their results. Their ongoing learning includes a balance of formal professional learning and informal, peer-to-peer collaborative learning. While their formal preparation to serve as coaches often introduces the basic knowledge, skills, and dispositions

successful coaches need, coaches make sense of that learning in their communities of practice. In their own learning communities, they share successes, challenges, and best practices. They discuss everyday challenges, such as helping staff understand the change process, developing productive team dynamics, working with different types of teachers, managing time and

> Coaches, like all educators, must continually improve their practice to better their results. Their ongoing learning includes a balance of formal professional learning and informal, peer-to-peer collaborative learning.

diverse responsibilities, establishing and maintaining trust, and measuring the effects of their work. They share examples of effective strategies, protocols, tools, refreshers, and other resources. Working as a community of practice to support each other's success also helps them model the importance of ongoing collaboration. By experiencing communities of practice as a routine part of their own work, coaches are better able to facilitate and support communities of practice in their schools.

Setting aside time for coaches to gain and maintain a repertoire of research-based practices and resources as they engage in collaborative learning is important for a successful coaching program, but out-of-building time often causes tension with teachers and principals. Principals want to maximize the time coaches spend with teachers. Teachers want to engage in professional learning with the coach and may question why coaches are pulled out of school for district-level professional learning. This tension requires that district and school leaders, teachers, and other stakeholders agree about the time required for coaches' learning. As coaching programs mature and coaches gain experience, districts sometimes are able to scale back the frequency of coaches' professional learning and other meetings.

Coach candidates must have the capacity to serve teachers as instructional leaders, grow professionally to learn how to coach, and have the flexibility and organizational skills to work in leadership roles.

Principal support

Principal support creates the conditions that give coaches the best opportunity to succeed: conditions such as clear expectations set with teachers about coaching to increase the coach's entrée to classrooms, a consistent focus on the school's improvement goals, and day-to-day supervision and guidance that help the coach meet teachers' diverse learning needs. When the coach and principal have good communication, the coach is supported and better able to attain jointly established goals.

Principal support is such a foundational aspect of the coach's work that a separate chapter is devoted to this relationship. See Chapter 9 for a detailed description of the support principals provide coaches.

External support

Coaches also benefit from external support from outside experts who work with coaching programs throughout the nation and provide ongoing professional learning as coaches mature in their role.

In addition, coaches expand their expertise and gain a broader perspective by networking with coach colleagues outside their district. Coaches who work in rural or small school districts with few coaches and limited internal support find networking especially beneficial. Interacting in electronic or face-to-face communities of practice within regions, states, provinces, or even internationally, coaches can reflect with peers about approaches to their work and learn strategies, share tools and resources, and expand their repertoires. Social networking, wikis, blogs, Twitter, LinkedIn, Pings, Nings, and other means of collaborating are excellent resources.

Coaches also can invest in professional learning through membership in professional associations that provide specific resources. Many associations have special resources for coaches, including online programs, meetings, conferences, and materials for those in teacher leadership or coaching roles.

Learning Forward resources for coaches

- *The Leading Teacher*

- Learning Forward's summer conference

- Learning Forward state affiliates with special programs for coaches

- Webinars (see www.learningforward.org)

Scenario

Clare Carter was a first-year, full-time instructional coach at Hilltop Elementary School. As she met for the first time with her assigned mentor before school began, the two focused on ways to make their relationship productive.

Brad Silva, her mentor, worked to build trust by asking Carter to share her expectations of him as her mentor and then by sharing his expectations for her. Silva modeled a partnership agreement conversation by discussing with Carter when, where, how long, and how frequently they would meet. Carter made a mental note of how important partnership agreement conversations are to productive, collaborative working relationships between coaches and teachers.

During the partnership agreement conversation, Carter prioritized her needs for support based on the district's expectations for her work, which included ensuring that all grade-level teams understood and used data and using student work to guide teachers' planning, and instruction. She also told Silva her school was focusing on literacy instruction. Carter said she needed Silva's help to find ways to build trust with the teachers in her building and get her foot in the door.

Silva told her about his first year as a coach and how he had helped teachers however he could as a resource provider during the first month of school. He also cautioned Carter that teachers can become comfortable with the coach as a resource provider, and he had found it hard to move out of the role. He said he had had to remind himself and those he worked with that his goal was to improve teaching and learning at the building level, and that while much of what he accomplished during that first month helped teachers and built their acceptance and trust, it did not change teacher practice or increase student learning.

Silva then explained other roles he used that provided more leverage for increasing teacher competence, particularly facilitating team data conversations early in the school year. He said that once he had helped teachers analyze data, he was able to co-plan instructional units with them, conduct demonstration lessons, co-teach, and ultimately pre-conference, observe the teachers, and provide post-observation conferences using data-based feedback.

Silva asked Carter to think carefully about how to approach her first week of school, emphasizing that all schools and teachers are different and that what he learned might not apply in Carter's school. Carter concluded that she wanted to offer to test students during the first week of school and help teachers find books, websites and other resources to support their instruction as they started their school year. She also vowed to move on quickly to the more rigorous work of grade-level data conversations around literacy. She told Silva she might need his help to find ways to say no to teachers who asked for continued resource services.

Carter asked if she could observe Silva in a grade-level data conversation. She also wanted to co-plan her data conversations. She wanted a meeting structure that ensured that all voices were heard and that team members listened to each other rather than advocating for their own interests. Silva offered to co-facilitate the first data conversation and to debrief with Carter afterward. He offered to observe her facilitating the second data conversation and provide feedback on her areas of concern.

Their first meeting helped Carter and Silva establish a foundation focused on Carter's desire to become an effective coach, improve teaching and learning in literacy, and support her colleagues by focusing on work that would make the greatest difference.

Reflection questions

- What is the value of coaches having mentors? Is it more important for new coaches to have mentors?

- How might your district or school be able to provide mentoring for coaches? Who might mentor?

- What special skills does Silva demonstrate as a new coach mentor? What makes those skills important for someone who mentors a new coach?

- What confidentiality issues arise in Carter's request of Silva to watch him in a grade-level meeting? How might these issues be different if the request had been to observe Silva in a one-on-one coaching conversation? What do you recommend that Carter and Silva do to mitigate these issues?

- How does the partnership agreement between Carter and Silva support their relationship?

Recommendations for

Central office administrators

- Identify enough coach champions so the ratio of coaches to champions is one full-time champion for each 20 to 25 teacher leaders to help ensure that coaches have support to solve problems. The coach champion's responsibilities should not be added on to an existing full-time job but should be a substantial and defined part of the champion's job.

- Establish the expectation that champions be on site and work with coaches at least once every month or six weeks; that they meet with the principal and teacher leader about three times per year; and that they attend training with teacher leaders.

- Support champions in helping coaches and principal set goals that align the coach's work with schoolwide areas of focus and have follow-up conferences to monitor the coach's success.

- Set the expectation that principals and champions are equal partners in giving teacher leaders feedback. Outline a process for principals to provide regular feedback to teacher leaders.

- Assign each novice to an expert or mentor teacher leader. Provide time and support for them to meet regularly.

- Expect that principals and coaches will discuss partnership agreements formally or informally early each school year and will communicate regularly.

- Identify a common curriculum for all teacher leaders so they develop the knowledge and skills they need to succeed. This curriculum should match their job description.

- Give administrators ongoing support and training in how to work effectively with coaches, including on-site support as needed.

- Provide ongoing, regular opportunities for coaches to meet and interact with each other to discuss challenges and to coach each other around problems of practice.

- Provide protocols to support meaningful interactions and regular time for coaches to communicate and share best practices.

- Educate others about the time coaches need for professional learning and create agreements maximizing the time coaches work directly with teachers.

Building administrators

- Define, communicate, and monitor the practice of confidentiality so all staff are uniformly versed in the rationale and importance of this practice.

- Meet frequently with coaches to discuss roles, goals, work, alignment, challenges, and results.

- Set clear expectations for all staff about working with coaches to improve instruction and student learning.
- Communicate partnership agreements between the principal and coach to staff members to increase transparency in the work.
- Revisit the partnership agreement frequently and revise it as needed.
- Support teacher engagement in coaching by coordinating schedules to allow teachers to meet with the coach.
- Give coaches time to engage in their own communities of practice and professional learning.

Coaches

- Establish and frequently review partnership agreements with principals.
- Communicate needs, requests, and feedback to the principal directly, openly, and factually.
- Support the principal as the school's primary instructional leader.
- Seek support from the principal when needed.
- Share successes, challenges, and best practices with other coaches during regularly scheduled meetings.
- Help the principal keep frequent communication a high priority by making communication easily accessible, flexible, and useful.

TOOL INDEX
Chapter 8

	TOOL	PURPOSE
8.1	**Consultancy protocol**	Look at and solve dilemmas as a team using this process.
8.2	**Success-analysis protocol**	Help individuals identify and describe successful practices using this protocol.
8.3	**Gap-analysis protocol**	Use this protocol to help teams identify current practices and create, expand, or extend an environment where successful practices can flourish.
8.4	**Problem-solving protocol**	Solve conflicts and other problems with this structured process.
8.5	**Resources**	Consult this list of websites for further reading and research.

To download tools, see www.learningforward.org/publications/coachingmatters

Principal-coach
relationships

The heart of a successful coaching program is the relationship between the principal and the coach. The principal serves as the school's primary instructional leader, and the coach shares and supports the principal's vision. Their partnership is crucial to successfully implementing the coaching program (Wren & Vallejo, 2009).

The principal and coach work hand in hand to make quality instruction a top priority and create a culture of collaboration and inquiry. Together, principals and coaches communicate their common belief that well-prepared teachers who consistently implement research-based instructional practices and continually strive to improve their practices make the greatest difference in student learning. This shared belief is a common indicator of an effective principal-coach relationship.

Effective principal-coach relationships are built on the key elements of: communication, feedback, expectations, time and resources, confidentiality, and professional development.

The coach and principal's communication is essential to implementing coaching effectively.

Communication

The coach and principal's communication is essential to implementing coaching effectively. When their working relationship begins, the effective coach and principal create a partnership agreement for how they will work together to carry out their shared vision for the school. The partnership agreement addresses the principal's and coach's expectations for:

- The coach's roles and responsibilities, as well as clients' roles and responsibilities;
- Desired outcomes of the coaching and coaching's alignment with school goals;
- Coaching's boundaries and limitations;
- How many and which teachers the coach will work with (preferably all teachers in the school);
- What procedures teachers will use to access the coach's services;
- Resources and support the coach needs to carry out the work;
- Ways to assess the coach's effectiveness;
- Confidentiality about teacher and coach interactions;
- Communication and reporting procedures; and
- Allocation of the coach's time and timelines for engaging in coaching.

During these partnership agreement conversations, the coach and the principal discuss how they will monitor the work and how often and when they will meet to share updates and to collaborate.

They make it a priority to meet for 30 minutes to an hour each week (Knight, 2007). Meeting weekly to plan and collaborate demonstrates the principal's and coach's belief that they can draw on each other's strengths and expertise to enhance their effectiveness in their respective roles. Their regular meetings help ensure their messages are aligned and reinforce each other's, and that they do not have different or unfair expectations of any teachers or teacher teams.

Coaches often worry that teachers view these meetings with the principal as reporting on teachers. They worry that they may inadvertently breach their confidentiality agreements in the natural course of their conversations with the principal. The principal and teachers must remain vigilant about the partnership agreements and speak up when confidentiality slips.

The coach and principal might use their regular meetings to discuss:

- Teachers: Which teachers the coach worked with in the past week, and with whom the coach plans to work in the upcoming week.
- Topics: Topics the coach is focusing on with teachers.
- Time: How much time the coach is spending with individuals and teams of teachers.
- Tasks: Tasks the coach is doing (for example, modeling, co-planning, conducting a data meeting, and so on).

The coach may have entered factual information in a log, so the principal and coach might review the week's entries. Coaches also use their weekly time with principals to share their own learning from their practice or from professional development with other coaches, to communicate information from district meetings that principals need to know, ask for the support they need to make their work more effective, and discuss any difficulties. If the coach feels that asking for support or solving a problem will breach confidentiality, the coach should seek support from the district coach champion rather than the principal.

Eventually, as coaches and principals work together over time and a culture of collaboration grows within a school, teachers will more routinely share information about their practices. When teachers, coaches, and principals are comfortable speaking openly about teaching and learning, the coach and principal can relax the strict agreements about confidentiality.

When either the coach or principal feels that the teachers are ready to move past strict controls

> Eventually, as coaches and principals work together over time and a culture of collaboration grows within a school, teachers will more routinely share information about their practices.

about confidentiality, they should not make the change on their own. They should gather the staff, propose changes to the confidentiality agreements, and engage teachers in the decision.

The principal's style is key to a coach's success

How the principal supports the coach influences how successful coaching and the coaching program will be. Jacy Ippolito (2009) identifies three styles of principal interaction with their coaches: neglectful, interfering, and partnering.

Neglectful principals may have high expectations, but for a variety of reasons, they do not follow through with the support coaches need. They may not adapt the school schedule, may not meet regularly with the coach, don't set priorities with staff about coaching, don't establish and keep a partnership agreement, fail to offer the coach continuous feedback, or don't align the coach's work with the school improvement plan.

Interfering principals, according to Ippolito, have a difficult time letting go of or sharing responsibility for professional development. They may usurp meeting agendas, may be directive about which teachers the coach works with, and may specify the topic of the coach's work. Interfering principals often unintentionally confuse teachers and even the coach, and they potentially undermine teachers' work.

Partnering principals provide leadership for coaching by setting high expectations, providing ongoing support to the coach, and providing feedback to the coach and staff about coaching. Ippolito notes that one way partnering principals support coaches is by modeling partnership and collaboration in all aspects of their work within the school and community. "[M]uch of this culture of collaboration and professional learning [can be attributed to] the partnering stance of the administration," says one coach in Ippolito's research (p. 3).

Feedback is essential

As part of the ongoing conversations between the principal and coach to monitor the process, the principal should maintain time to offer the coach explicit feedback about the coach's effectiveness. The coach may ask the principal for specific feedback about an activity, or the feedback may be about routine components of the coach's work.

Whether the principal or a district-level administrator is the coach's formal supervisor, the coach still needs regular feedback. The principal often is well informed about the coach's work because the principal participates in professional development sessions with the coach and faculty and also visits classrooms. The principal can see how the coach's work is affecting

> When the principal and the coach have established professional respect and trust, the coach will look forward to receiving the principal's feedback and having an opportunity to make adjustments to the work to be able to affect teachers' practice even more.

teachers' practices as well as the school's culture and climate. When the principal and the coach have established professional respect and trust, the coach will look forward to receiving the principal's feedback and having an opportunity to make adjustments to the work to be able to affect teachers' practices even more.

Set clear expectations

The principal's ability to set clear expectations for teachers about how they will work with the coach significantly affects the coach's work. Principals often assume either that coaches will work with teachers who need the most help or that coaches will work with all the teachers in the school. When the principal doesn't make the expectation public to both the staff and the coach, the expectation frequently goes unmet. Establishing expectations that define how much and how teachers will work with the coach enables the coach to partner with teachers and avoid potential tension and conflict.

The principal is responsible for monitoring and holding teachers accountable for meeting the expectation. If the principal identifies a teacher who might benefit from working with the coach, often because the teacher's performance is substandard in some area, the principal is responsible for making known to the teacher that the teacher needs the coach's support. The principal holds the teacher accountable for improving his or her practice and allows the coach to maintain a supportive rather than evaluative role. If the teacher is aware of the principal's expectations, the teacher's work with the coach can be more focused.

Often, however, principals allow teachers to choose to work with the coach. Teachers who can choose how they will work with a coach usually are more invested in the work than those who have no choice (Knight, 2007).

Overall, principals' behaviors affect coaching, teachers' engagement in coaching, and the coach. Researchers correlated teachers' participation in coaching and principals' support behaviors and found that teachers are more likely to participate in coaching when the principal:
- Treats coaches as valued professionals;
- Publicly endorses the coach as a content expert;

- Actively participates in the content-focused coaching program; and
- Provides overall support to the coach in all categories of principal support.
(Matsumura et al., 2009)

The principal shows support for coaching by being involved and engaged. Visible support paves the way for the coach to work more effectively with teachers. For example, when a principal attends some of the grade-level or department meetings that the coach facilitates or engages in professional development alongside teachers, the principal conveys the message that these activities are worthwhile.

Teachers participate in coaching less when coaches and principals have a less consistent understanding of the work that coaches do and of what support principals provide coaches (Matsumura et al., 2009).

As the principal sets expectations for the coach's role, the principal must be careful not to rely on the coach for managerial tasks that can take away from the coach's ability to add to the school's instructional leadership. In a Florida study of middle school literacy coaches, district supervisors reported that coaches were occasionally expected to serve as substitute teachers or administrators (Marsh et al., 2008).

The coach's impact is greatly diminished if the coach spends time on noncoaching duties. In the Florida study, nearly 18% of coaches reported spending between six hours and 16 hours over a two-week period on noncoaching, administrative

Principal sends clear message

A principal might set a schoolwide expectation that all teachers work with the school's coach by sending a message such as:

One of the expectations we share at this school is that all students will succeed. We also believe that each of us has a responsibility to contribute to that success. We are fortunate to have Charles as our coach. Charles' primary role is to ensure that all students succeed, and he will work with each of you so that you engage in continuous professional learning to refine teaching practices so that we reach every student. As a part of your professional growth and collaboration, each teacher will work with Charles individually and also during your grade-level collaboration time. As a school, we will focus our professional growth on differentiating instruction to meet the learning needs of all students.

As teams and individuals, you will determine how Charles can help you meet the goals we have established for our school. Charles will work primarily as an instructional specialist, classroom supporter, and data coach, yet he has considerable latitude within those roles for the type of support he provides, and you will work together with him to determine what will best serve your learning needs.

As a professional and member of our school community, engaging in professional growth with Charles is not negotiable because we need all of us learning and working together in order to meet the needs of the students we serve.

duties, and 26% reported managing reading resources, budgeting, ordering, and overseeing computer software and reading laboratories (Marsh et al., 2008). While these tasks may contribute to a successful literacy program, they leave less time for a coach to focus on individual and team-based work with teachers to improve teaching and student learning. Judicious allocation of a coach's time in ways that are most likely to impact overall student achievement is a hallmark of an effective principal.

Modeling the value of professional learning for all staff members helps establish a culture of inquiry, learning, and continuous growth needed for schools to improve.

Align time and resources

Clear expectations for teachers' and coaches' collaboration alone are not enough, however. Principals who want to see results from coaching set up structures that align with the expectations. If the principal expects the coach to work with teacher teams, for example, the principal needs to give teachers a common planning period during the workday or workweek. If teachers use materials and technology in their work, they may need broadband access or other resources such as research or information related to their areas of inquiry. Principals sometimes can allocate funds to hire substitute teachers and release a team for a day of intensive planning. These kinds of support tell teachers that the principal is willing to invest in improvement, believes in their professionalism, and supports their work with the coach.

Over time, as the coaching program matures and teachers' comfort with coaching grows, the focus of the coach's work may change. The needs of staff and students then define how the coach allocates time. The coach can maintain a log to record and analyze how she spends her time and review the log periodically with the principal to ensure that her use of time aligns with the coaching program's goals and the school's improvement plan. When coaches and principals compare the coach's allocation of time to what is desired or needed, they can talk about any adjustments that may be needed to achieve their identified goals.

The coach's role is complex and multifaceted, and coaches, too, need ongoing professional development. Principals need to schedule time for the coach to attend district or other professional development sessions, even when the sessions occur during the school day and the coach needs to leave the building. The principal should communicate to teachers that the coach's professional learning is linked to the staff's professional learning, and that the principal expects the coach to share what he is learning with the entire staff. Modeling the value of professional learning for all staff members helps establish a culture of inquiry, learning, and continuous growth needed for schools to improve.

Ensure confidentiality

Having an explicit understanding that the coach's work does not influence teachers' evaluations increases the coach's chances of establishing relationships based on trust and confidence. If teachers perceive that the coach talks to the principal about teachers' practices, they are less likely to want to work with the coach or to see the coach as a support (Killion & Harrison, 2006).

An astute coach deliberately and systematically discusses confidentiality with all administrators and with teachers when establishing partnership agreements. The agreements specifically state that the coach will not share any information with administrators that could influence the administrators' evaluations of teachers. The only time a coach would share information with an administrator about a specific classroom action is if students' safety — physical, academic, or emotional — were in jeopardy

As the school's primary instructional leader, the principal is responsible for being visible in teachers' classrooms and being aware of each teacher's strengths and areas for growth. A principal who spends time formally observing in classrooms as well as informally dropping in on teachers on a regular basis will not expect the coach to assess teachers' strengths and needs.

Learn side by side

In many school districts, the central office designs and coordinates the coaching program, and coaches are expected to support district-level initiatives. Coaches help teachers implement the district's new programs or curricula, or they carry out the district's vision for school improvement. Ultimately, principals are responsible for teachers' implementing new programs and initiatives and for supporting coaches' work with teachers.

Both coaches and principals need professional development to carry out these tasks. The school and the district benefit when coaches and principals learn together about these initiatives so each clearly understands the other's scope of responsibility and they can agree on how to support one another's efforts. When the coach and principal sit side by side as they learn about a new initiative, they are able to determine how best to integrate the new program in their school's context. They can discern how the initiative relates to their shared vision for the school and how to engage other staff members in carrying out the vision. By attending professional development together, the coach and principal model the collaboration they want to encourage among the staff in order to create a culture of collaboration and inquiry that results in improved student learning.

In some schools and districts, the coach may plan and implement school-based professional

> The coach and principal model the collaboration they want to encourage among the staff.

development for teachers, either in small groups or individually. When districts create professional development for coaches that is data driven and based on a needs analysis, coaches are able to use effective designs to plan teachers' professional learning and determine how and when to use various designs. Taking part in quality professional development equips coaches to make good decisions about how to engage their colleagues.

Coaches seldom are the sole drivers of learning in their schools, however. The principal remains the school's primary instructional leader (Wren & Vallejo, 2009), and the coach shares expertise in pedagogy, curriculum content, and adult learning theory to support teachers in becoming more resourceful in their own classrooms. The principal may help the coach plan a session, may facilitate or co-facilitate, or may participate. When the principal models a professional, collaborative relationship with the coach for the staff, the principal is setting the tone for the culture of inquiry desired among staff members.

Scenario

Ranell Williams is a second-year coach in a large elementary school. During her first year, she focused mainly on mentoring three novice teachers on the staff, providing all teachers with resources, and helping teachers become more data savvy. At the beginning of the current year, Williams and the principal, Demond Davies, revisited the partnership agreement they had developed the previous year and adjusted how Williams would allocate her time, as well as how they would work together. They decided that Williams might have a greater effect on improving instruction if she met regularly with all grade-level teams. They talked about what teachers might focus on in their team meetings and Williams' role in facilitating those meetings. They discussed how Williams' work aligned with the school's improvement goals. They then settled on a schedule of two meetings each month with each team that Williams would facilitate and discussed a process for determining how the agenda would be set for each meeting to include input from the team members, as well as Williams' ideas.

Williams and Davies also talked about the dynamics of each team and what Williams might expect regarding teachers' engagement in regular team meetings and collaborative dialogue focused on teaching and learning. In the past, most teams had spent their meeting time talking about management issues rather than instructional issues. Williams found it helpful to hear Davies' perspective about these teams and appreciated that his comments were constructive and not focused on specific teachers or teams. She also appreciated his advice about how to help teams become stronger learning communities.

The pair agreed it was important that teachers knew what was expected of them in their learning community meetings. Davies promised that at the next faculty meeting he would clarify with the staff what he wanted to have happen. He also committed to attending some of each team's meetings throughout the year. He thought it would be helpful for Williams to begin working with the teams and put some norms and procedures into place with each group before he attended. They created a simple template that could be used at each meeting to describe the meeting's focus, outcomes planned, resources requested, results achieved, and next steps. Both of them thought that the template would be useful in monitoring Williams' work with the teams over time. Williams agreed to bring copies of the completed form to their weekly meetings to talk about her work and to plan together. Williams left this meeting feeling energized and hopeful that her work would make a greater difference in the coming year.

Reflection questions

- What are the possible outcomes of a school-based coach and the school's principal not having a clear partnership agreement or a good relationship?

- What are the top requirements in a principal and coach partnership agreement? Why did you identify these areas as priorities?

- How does Davies demonstrate his support of the coach and coaching?

- What strategies can coaches use to increase principal support of coaching and the coach?

- If the principal and coach have a strong relationship, as is evident between Williams and Davies, what benefits and disadvantages would they face in minimizing the number of meetings they have with each other?

Recommendations for

Central office administrators

- Design professional learning for coaches that includes how to work collaboratively with the principal.
- Plan and deliver joint professional learning for school-based coaches and principals about new programs or initiatives when coaches will be expected to support teachers in implementing the program or initiative.
- Convene coaches and principals before school begins to help them understand partnership agreements and write an agreement.
- Meet with coaches and their principals periodically during the school year to review their collaboration, assess whether they are communicating frequently and keeping their agreements, and determine whether they are collecting evidence of the coach's impact.

Building administrators

- Develop a partnership agreement with the coach to clarify expectations for the coach's work and for how administrators and the coach will work together. Revisit the agreement periodically.
- Include the topic of confidentiality in the partnership agreement.
- Define the respective roles of the principal and the coach in providing instructional leadership for the school.
- Communicate clear expectations to the staff regarding the coach's work.
- Communicate the principal and coach partnership agreement to the staff.
- Allocate time in the teachers' workday for them to work with the coach.
- Budget for material resources to support the coach's work.
- Set a regular time in the principal's schedule to meet with the coach to plan and review the coach's work.
- Offer the coach regular feedback.
- Attend district professional development with the coach when the coach is asked to support a new program or initiative with teachers.
- Become knowledgeable or maintain knowledge of what constitutes effective professional development.

Coaches

- Develop a partnership agreement with the principal to clarify expectations for coaching and how you will work together.
- Include the topic of confidentiality in the partnership agreement.
- Plan time for a regular meeting with the principal to monitor coaching's effect.
- Be receptive to feedback about coaching's impact and adjust behaviors as needed based on the feedback.
- Attend district professional development with the principal when you are asked to support a new program or initiative with teachers.

TOOL INDEX
Chapter 9

	TOOL	PURPOSE
9.1	**Instructional coach contact log template**	Maintain records of how the coach's time is allocated using this template.
9.2	**Sample partnership agreement between instructional coach and principal**	Define the working relationship between the coach and principal and the expectations for the coach's work with this sample partnership agreement.
9.3	**Partnership agreement map for instructional coach and principal**	Use this template as a basis for establishing agreements between the instructional coach and the principal regarding the coach's work.
9.4	**Partnership agreement example**	Study this example of an actual partnership agreement between an instructional coach and principal.
9.5	**Agreement of confidentiality**	Read this tool that defines and describes the importance of agreements about confidentiality.
9.6	**Testimonials from school-based instructional coaching program clients**	Use these excerpted comments from focus group participants in the evaluation of a coaching program to provide persuasive evidence for a coaching program.
9.7	**Coach's time chart**	Fill in this chart to track how you use your time during the week.

To download tools, see www.learningforward.org/publications/coachingmatters

Teacher-coach
relationships

I f the principal-coach relationship is the heart of the program, the teacher-coach relationship is the hands. Without a good relationship with teachers, coaches cannot get the work done.

To have a productive relationship, teachers and coaches need to trust one another, respect each other professionally, commit to keeping their partnership agreements, and clearly define the work they will do together. Teachers must believe that the coach supports them and that the coach's top priority is student academic achievement. The coach must believe that teachers are committed to continuous improvement and that teachers' top priority is student academic achievement. The mutual respect and professional focus of the coach-teacher relationship minimizes personal factors that may detract from a productive relationship.

Build relationships with teachers

Building strong, productive relationships with teachers requires six key elements:

- Creating effective partnership agreements;
- Building teacher leadership capacity;
- Communicating about coaching services;
- Allowing teachers to identify their needs and to choose how a coach provides support (allowing teachers "a voice and a choice");
- Encouraging feedback; and
- Managing resistance and conflict.

Creating effective agreements

To have a constructive and productive relationship, teachers and coaches agree in advance on how they will work together and the kind of work they will do. An agreement reduces teachers' anxiety about what the coaching experience is and creates a foundation for a trusting relationship.

A coach may want a partnership agreement with individual teachers and with teams of teachers. Partnership agreements often describe each party's roles and responsibilities, outline desired outcomes for the work, define how the work will be measured, specify what data the coach and teacher will examine and how they will follow up, describe what the coach and the teacher need from one another to be successful, tell how they will interact with one another, and spell out what is confidential.

One of the most important aspects of partnership-agreement conversations teachers and coaches have is about what confidentiality means in their relationship. The coach is more likely to be able to establish trust and gain teachers' confidence if everyone explicitly understands that the coach's work does not influence the principal's evaluation of teachers in any way or affect the principal's regard for the teachers. If teachers think the coach tells the principal about their practices, they are less inclined to want to work with the coach or to see the coach as a support. Coaches and teachers can negotiate what is permissible to share with other teachers or the administrator.

An astute coach discusses the bounds of confidentiality with administrators as well as with teachers when establishing partnership agreements. Conversations about partnership agreements allow teachers to share how they might work most effectively with the coach and what specific needs they have. The coach may want to use an agenda or conversation map to focus the conversation. A summary restatement ending the conversation ensures that the teacher and coach agree on the specifics of the working relationship.

Usually both the parties write and sign the partnership agreement, but the agreement also can be less formal, such as having one person, usually the coach, take notes during the conversation and copy the notes for the other person.

Partnership agreements are not stagnant — they evolve as the relationship between the coach and teacher evolves. Early on, when the coach and teacher are more tentative about the relationship, the agreements are clear and explicit. As the relationship matures and becomes more focused, businesslike, and intentional, the agreements, while never ignored, may require less focus.

Building teacher leadership capacity

One indicator that coaching is effective is when teacher leadership grows. Coaches are not the only teacher leaders at a school site. Coaches who see it as their responsibility to develop teacher leadership send the message that all teachers have leadership potential and responsibilities. These coaches see themselves as models of leadership practices and make their practices transparent so that other teachers can learn to coach. Teachers are more engaged when coaches demonstrate respect for teachers' knowledge and practices.

Guiding questions for partnership agreement conversations

These questions can help guide coaches forming partnership agreements with individual teachers, with teaching teams, and when they visit the classroom:

Partnership agreements with an individual teacher

- What do you want to accomplish in our work together?

- What services can I provide that will help you accomplish this end?

- What are the best ways for us to work together?

- When will we work together?

- What resources will be helpful in our work? Who will bring those resources?

- How long do we expect this to take?

- How will we know if we are successful?

Partnership agreements for a team meeting

- What do you hope to learn when we work together?

- What do you want the result of this meeting to be?

- What is the focus of our work together?

- What services from me will be most beneficial to you?

- How shall we work together today? What role do you want me to play — responder, peer, expert, critical friend, or another role?

- When shall I meet you and where?

- What resources will you bring to our meeting? What would you like me to bring?

- Who else will we involve in this work?

- When and how long will our subsequent meetings be?

- What time is best for us to work together?

When I observe in your class, what data do you want me to gather?

- What are your classroom rules?

- Which students will be particularly noticeable today?

- What areas do you want feedback on?

- Where should I sit when I am in your room observing? May I interact with students during my visit, or do you prefer that I not?

- Where shall we meet for our feedback session?

- What time shall we meet for our feedback session?

- How long will our meeting be?

A conversation about a partnership agreement

A conversation might sound like this:

Agenda item 1: Focus on the method of support the coach provides.

Coach: Let's take a few minutes to review our partnership agreements.

Teacher: OK. I didn't know we had any agreements.

Coach: Last time we worked together, you said that you wanted me to give you strategies to address specific problems. I also remember that you wanted me to be more direct with you rather than to beat around the bush by asking lots of questions. I recall you asking me to give you several strategies for each area we discussed and asking that I help you know which one fit best with your class and the content. Is this still how you prefer for us to work?

Teacher: Yes, although this time I want you to help me identify those strategies to see if I can figure out on my own what to do. Of course, I want your ideas, too. I want us to change our working agreement this time in this way. I hope this works for you.

Coach: Yes, of course. I help you generate ideas, and then if you want me to add strategies to your list, I will. I hope that we continue to talk about how to select a strategy and evaluate its effectiveness.

Teacher: Yes, I definitely want to do that.

Coach: Great. Now let's also review the 9th-grade writing team goal for this six-week period so that we have that in front of us, and then we can talk specifically about our work together now that we know how we will collaborate.

Agenda item 2: Focus on the content of the support the coach provides.

Coach: Your team said that during this six-week period, teachers wanted to increase students' performance in writing introductions from an average of 2.3 on the writing rubric to an average of 3.0 out of 4.0. In our last round of coaching, we talked about a various introductions, and you were going to practice having students write introductions. How did your students do?

Teacher: I can see improvement. However, I'm not confident that my students are doing more than mechanical writing. They don't have voice or personality in their introductions — no emotion or anything to draw in readers. I don't know how to get that from them. If we scored their introductions, you would see that the introductions are fine and probably all meeting the three expectations, but the writing does nothing for me.

Coach: I can tell you want more from your students and that you also think they are capable of more, so you want to think about how to get their voices into their writing. You acknowledge that they have improved, and yet you see room for more growth.

Teacher: Definitely. How does a teacher teach something so abstract?

A conversation about a partnership agreement (cont'd)

Coach: We can explore that together if you want.

Teacher: I'd like that.

Coach: Let's set a goal for our own learning about how to incorporate voice in student writing, particularly in introductions, so that readers are more immediately engaged and students' writing incorporates their personalities and voice. How would we know, say in six weeks, that we met this goal?

Agenda item 3: Focus on confidentiality.

Coach: I want to reiterate my commitment to keeping our coaching sessions confidential. What that means to me is that I won't talk to others about what I observe in your classroom or the specifics of what you and I discuss. I will, for the purpose of reporting, record that I worked with you and how we worked together. For example, if I co-teach with you, I will write down the amount of time I spend with you and identify the topic. I might write: Jess Brown, co-planning for lesson, 30 minutes; co-teaching lesson on fractions, 45 minutes; and debriefing lesson, 30 minutes.

Teacher: Thanks for that reminder. Sometimes I wonder if it would help all of us on the 9th-grade team if you shared what each of us is doing with you. Does this mean that you won't do that?

Coach: I won't share what I am doing with you specifically. However, I want you to feel comfortable sharing the information in team meetings if you want to. I encourage you to ask your colleagues about what they are doing. I am bound by my agreement of confidentiality not to share this information unless, as a team, you all want to change the agreement so that we can talk only among ourselves about the work we are doing as a team. I agree with you that it would help you all become more collaborative and discover that you each have information to share with one another. I'd encourage you to initiate a conversation with your colleagues about this at our meeting next Tuesday. Let me know if you want help planning how to bring it up in the meeting.

Teacher: Thanks. I will.

Coaches can foster teacher leadership in many ways. Coaches can:

- Invite other teachers to facilitate a team meeting, and guide and support novice facilitators.
- Seek other teachers' support with complex challenges related to student learning and teaching.
- Invite teachers to add resources, examples, models, or ideas to conversations.
- Invite teachers to discuss their instructional decisions so that others understand the theoretical, research, or contextual rationale for the decision.
- Use reflection protocols to foster reflection.
- Encourage teachers to present in critical friends' groups.
- Encourage teachers to facilitate professional development for their peers.

- Provide professional development in teacher leadership skills for interested teachers.
- Coach team, grade-level, or department chairs on their leadership skills.
- Share practices or resources with designated teacher leaders or those who want to develop their leadership capacity.
- Pair teachers as peer observers to provide each other feedback.
- Engage teachers in walk-throughs or instructional rounds to gather data about teaching and learning, and participate in debriefing sessions.
- Invite teachers to serve as hosts for walk-throughs or instructional rounds.
- Encourage teachers to open their classrooms to other teachers to visit.

Some teachers hesitate to take leadership roles, seeing the challenge as adding responsibilities to their regular work. Others consider leadership responsibilities only as a track to school administration. However, schools today have enough leadership opportunities and forms of leadership to allow just about any interested teacher to lead in some way. Coaches also can help create leadership opportunities for teachers who prefer to remain in the classroom.

Coaching is most successful when instruction improves, student learning increases — and more teachers see themselves as leaders.

To build teachers' confidence as they step into leadership roles, coaches apply the same gradual-release principle they use in coaching instruction to build leadership expertise — I do, we do, you do. As teachers gain confidence, they can gradually assume some of the coach's responsibilities so that eventually the coach can shift responsibilities or assume new ones. Other teacher leaders can take over roles including data coach, learning facilitator, instructional specialist, and more. When teacher leaders are active within a school and assume leadership responsibilities, their sense of collegiality is stronger, they feel more engaged and professional, and they have a greater effect on student achievement.

Coaching is most successful when instruction improves, student learning increases — and more teachers see themselves as leaders and contributors to the professionalism within their schools.

Communicating about coaching services

Coaches can encourage teachers to participate in coaching by communicating which coaching services are offered. What the coach can provide and the coach's availability depend on the coaching program's goals and parameters. For example, if a district has determined that its coaches will serve as data coaches, instructional and curriculum specialists, and learning facilitators, the coach will need to provide services associated with those roles. So a data coach would meet with teachers individually or in teams to analyze student data and also might help the principal facilitate whole-school faculty meetings to review data about student achievement, engagement, demographics, perceptions, and so on. Some coaches have surveyed staff and then outlined services that respond to teacher needs.

Coaches have different ways of letting teachers know what support is available. Some coaches have created electronic or print menus listing the coach's support options. Others

Teacher Leader Model Standards

The Teacher Leader Model Standards provide coaches with guidance to facilitate teacher leadership among their colleagues and describe teacher leader functions. The standards describe seven domains of leadership, each of which is supported by a list of functions that a teacher leader who is an expert in that domain might perform:

Domain I: Fostering a collaborative culture to support educator development and student learning

Domain II: Accessing and using research to improve practice and student learning

Domain III: Promoting professional learning for continuous improvement

Domain IV: Facilitating improvements in instruction and student learning

Domain V: Promoting the use of assessments and data for school and district improvement

Domain VI: Improving outreach and collaboration with families and community

Domain VII: Advocating for student learning and the profession

Source: www.teacherleaderstandards.org.

have created one-page descriptions or brochures (see Chapter 5 tools). Some approaches are creative; others are more straightforward. The form of the communication sends a message about how the coach intends teachers to view coaching.

In almost all of these communication tools, coaches include details such as how to connect with the coach and the best way, whether by email, a note in the coach's mailbox, or with a phone message. Written or electronic formats generally include a place for the teacher's name and a spot to check off the requested service. These communication tools help a coach prepare and be ready to focus when working with teachers. Teachers then can consider in advance how to benefit from the coach's support, which increases their engagement, intentionality, and, potentially, the results.

In addition to communicating the services they offer, coaches periodically report to the staff, principals, and the coach champion which services they have provided. Most coaching programs require coaches to complete some form of log (see Chapter 9 tools) that the coaching program director and school principal use to manage the program.

Teachers often wonder how coaches spend their time when the coach is not with a particular team or individual teacher. To keep teachers informed, coaches can create a summary to share with all staff — a circle graph of how the coach's time is allocated or a description of the amount of time the coach spent in various services. The data can be pulled easily from the coach's log. The summary could be included in the staff newsletter, shared in a faculty meeting or school leadership team meeting, or posted on the faculty Web page. By seeing this information, teachers may get ideas about how to benefit from coaching services in the future.

Allowing teachers a voice and choice

Teachers can't be forced to engage in coaching. A more positive approach is to set clear expectations and allow teachers to identify their needs and choose the services the coach provides and

When coaches actively seek feedback and use it for professional growth, they model professional behavior — continuous learning.

the focus of the coach-teacher interaction. Giving teachers a voice and choice empowers and respects the voice of teachers (Knight, 2007). Choice means believing "that teachers should have choice regarding what and how they learn" (Knight, 2007, p. 41).

When teachers are respected and given choice in their professional learning and the professional learning the coach provides aligns more closely with teachers' unique needs, teachers are more likely to perceive value in the coaching and apply what they learn from the coach.

As principals convey expectations about coaching, it is important that they expect that teachers take an active role in the coaching process by clarifying the specific type of support they want and their goal for the coaching interaction.

The coach's role is to create a trusting, collaborative relationship with teachers to make the process inviting, to listen deeply, to seek to understand teachers' needs, and to support them in meeting their individual, team, school, and district goals.

Encouraging feedback

Another strategy to engage teachers as willing partners in coaching is to encourage and expect teachers to give the coach feedback. Teachers' feedback focuses on what the coach is doing to

enhance — and hinder — teachers' learning. When coaches actively seek feedback and use it for professional growth, they model professional behavior — continuous learning.

Coaches also might ask for feedback in the form of what changes teachers are making in their own practices and what changes they see in student learning. When teachers can articulate the effects of coaching, coaches use the information to reflect on how effective their coaching has been. Coaches can get regular feedback by asking teachers:

- What recommendations do you have for me as a coach?
- What did I do in our work today and in other coaching interactions that hindered your learning?
- What did I do in our work today and in other coaching interactions that helped your learning?
- What would you like me to continue doing?
- What would you like me to stop doing?
- What worked today and during other coaching interactions? What didn't?
- What do you suggest I do to improve?
- What changes are you making in your teaching as a result of coaching?
- What do you notice changing for your students as a result of changes in your teaching?

In addition to gathering feedback about the effectiveness of their coaching, coaches also may want to consider what teachers are reporting about changes in their practices and student learning. Asking questions periodically in individual or team coaching sessions gives coaches information and teachers an opportunity to reflect. Information about what teachers are actually implementing gives coaches information on whether they are providing adequate support for implementation. Ask:

- What changes are you making in your teaching as a result of coaching?
- What do you notice changing for your students as a result of changes in your practice?

In addition to informal feedback, coaches can ask for anonymous feedback using periodic surveys to collect teachers' opinions of the coaching program and the coach's services. While coaches use the informal feedback themselves, the principal or coaching program director might want to use survey data in a formative or summative assessment of the coaching program and the coach.

However coaches get feedback, they need specific feedback to be able to improve their coaching practices and become more effective.

Managing resistance and conflict

Despite a coach's best efforts to engage with teachers as a trusted colleague, not every teacher — even when there is a schoolwide or districtwide expectation for coaching — is willing to have coaching support. Teachers resist coaching for many reasons. They may falsely assume that the coach will focus on deficits rather than continuous development. They may fear being found inadequate or may be reluctant to make their practice public. Sometimes resistance is the result of a previous experience or a personal difference with the coach.

Resistance also has varying degrees. It may be slight and easily overcome. Sometimes, however, resistance is more subversive and can damage the potential for a long-term, collaborative relationship. It can be bold and overt, making the coach or teachers uncomfortable and inviting other teachers to choose sides. Examples of more severe resistance include:

- Repeated incidents of the teacher forgetting he or she was scheduled to work with the coach;
- Frequently being late to meetings with the coach;
- Repeatedly not using new practices; and
- Avoiding the coach.

Coaches may find it easier to avoid confronting resisters, but doing so conveys that the coach may not have noticed the resister or is not valuing that person, or that the coach is unwilling to support all teachers. The resisting teacher may be trying to prove just this idea. Avoiding the matter also may model the same behaviors the resisting teacher is modeling, defeating the coach's goal of improving the relationship.

Resistance requires effort to resolve, yet putting forth that extra effort often is what the coach least feels like doing. The coach has better leverage to address resistance in most cases, however, because unlike those in supervisory roles, the coach can work with the resisting teacher in a nonthreatening way with no consequences for the teacher.

Engaging with rather than avoiding a resisting teacher is the coach's best first step. Engagement can range from being genuinely friendly to asking for help. Being cordial can include greeting the teacher, talking about nonteaching-related

> Engaging with rather than avoiding a resisting teacher is the coach's best first step.

topics, and involving the teacher in conversations with others. Another approach — asking the teacher for advice or assistance — models that the coach is a learner, is willing to seek assistance, and is open to receiving it. If possible, the

Overcoming resistance

A brief excerpt from an interaction between a coach and a teacher illustrates how deep listening can help to overcome a teacher's resistance:

8th-grade teacher: I can't imagine why anyone would think it is possible that all 8th-grade students can pass Algebra I. I would have to make failing work worth a C and C work an A to even get close to that. Some of these students just aren't ready for the work.

Coach: High standards of learning are important for the success of all students. It is clear to me that you have high standards for student learning in your classroom.

8th-grade teacher: I do, but my students' scores are the lowest in the entire school. I have the lowest group of students. There is no way for all of them to pass.

Coach: Students learn in different ways and at different levels. I wonder if you recall a student you did not think would pass and who surprised you. I'd like to hear what you did to help that student succeed.

coach should report back to the teacher how the teacher's advice helped.

Many coaches take too much responsibility for the resistance. A coach often is not the cause of the resistance and is more often the object of it. Coaches should try to understand what is behind the teacher's resistance, the underlying cause of it. Getting to the bottom of the cause may require deep listening. Coaches listen for the resisting teacher's passion and priorities, dissect complaints, and turn complaints into desires. When coaches use skillful communication involving deep listening and noninvasive questioning, they may be able to bridge the resistance gap.

However, if the resistance becomes destructive, the coach may need the principal to step in and take supervisory actions.

Conflict, too, is inevitable in any relationship, especially when values and results are involved. Teachers and coaches will experience conflicts with one another, as will principals and coaches. Conflict can be addressed constructively or destructively.

Coaches need strong conflict resolution skills to address problem as they arise so any issues do not interrupt improvement efforts. An effective problem-solving process can help to prevent minor disagreements from becoming major conflicts. The process includes asking participants to identify their interests, detail what is important to them in this situation rather than their positions, and suggest solutions. When both parties focus on interests, they are more likely to find mutually acceptable options that will help resolve the issue. As when coaches face resistance, ignoring conflicts or minimizing their importance may have a long-term, negative effect on relationships.

When the coach is unable to address a conflict successfully, she or he may turn for help to the principal or district coaching program supervisor. If the conflict is with a principal, the coach may want to use a neutral party or third-party mediator from outside the school to facilitate the conversation if the coach feels less able to resolve the matter with someone who has supervisory authority. Sometimes the coach just may want to be coached on how to handle the situation rather than having a mediator. Districts need to make available whatever help a coach wants in order to address conflict in these important interactions.

Take a rotation approach to coaching

Coaches often are challenged to get teachers to request help. Principals can help bypass this challenge by setting clear expectations for how teachers are to engage in coaching and creating regular schedules for the coach to work with individuals and teams of teachers. Any plan for how the coach allocates time is a joint decision between the coach and principal and should align with the school's improvement plan.

Many schools create a regular rotation schedule in which the coach works with a grade-level team, teaching team, department, or other group for a week at a time. The coach meets with the team and each individual teacher at least once. If the teachers cannot meet for a block of time during that week, the coach might meet with the team during common planning periods over several days.

During the rest of each day, the coach has time to meet with teachers outside the team who have asked for immediate help and cannot wait until their regular rotation. The coach also has time to meet with the principal to plan and to manage recordkeeping. In addition, coaches might dedicate a portion of time each week to work with novice teachers.

The success of a rotation approach to coaching depends on clear expectations and the coach's commitment to meet with the team and individual teachers.

If the school does not use a rotation schedule, the coach might ask teachers to request coaching.

Having teachers initiate requests for coaching alleviates the perception that coaching is meant to "fix" a teacher in need of improvement. Coaches want to reinforce the idea that coaching helps all teachers continue to grow professionally and to gain new skills to meet new challenges. When principals direct coaches to work with particular teachers because the principal believes the teacher has inadequacies, the coach's objectivity may be compromised. In addition, the principal may expect the coach then to report back on how the teacher is improving. Allowing teachers to initiate coaching avoids any misinterpretation about why a coach is supporting a teacher.

To avoid the perception that a teacher requesting coaching lacks skills, the principal may require all teachers to work with the coach and hold teachers accountable for receiving coaching. Establishing procedures for teachers to initiate requests for coaching mitigates the occasional misinterpretation about coaching's purpose and engages teachers in expressing their willingness and openness to be coached, an important first

> To avoid the perception that a teacher requesting coaching lacks skills, the principal may require all teachers to work with the coach and hold teachers accountable for receiving coaching.

step in the change process. As all teachers engage with the coach, staff build a healthy culture of collaboration in which every educator is committed to learning and growing to best meet student needs.

Zenia Escobar, an elementary coach for five years at a high-needs school, is passionate about helping the students at her school. At times, in fact, her zeal can be overwhelming to the point that some of her peers perceive her as offensive.

Last year, Escobar had conversations with nearly all the teachers and formed partnership agreements with them. For the most part, these conversations went well. One notable exception was the conversation with Jeanine Thompson, a 3rd-grade teacher. Thompson was a veteran teacher and one of the original members of the school faculty when the school opened 10 years ago.

During a subsequent meeting with the 3rd-grade teachers, Escobar became frustrated and implied that this group of teachers, and especially Thompson, were not working hard enough to meet all students' needs. As a result of that meeting, Thompson refused to meet again with Escobar, even though the principal made it clear that all teachers were to work with the coach.

When the principal learned about the situation from Thompson's fellow teachers, he asked Escobar and Thompson to come to his office together to work out their issues. After 15 to 20 minutes of hard conversation, it was clear that the tension was caused by the two educators' differing expectations for students and their underlying assumptions about who was primarily responsible for student achievement. Escobar placed the responsibility squarely with teachers, while Thompson believed it was impossible for teachers to overcome all of the deficiencies students came with due to poverty and family backgrounds.

Escobar suggested that she co-teach with each of the 3rd-grade teachers to demonstrate strategies that might be more effective with some of their hard-to-motivate students. By the end of the conversation,

Scenario

it seemed that Escobar and Thompson had identified roles each would take as they worked together with the 3rd-grade students.

A week later, Thompson and Escobar had a planning conversation to design a lesson they would co-teach about fractions and their decimal equivalents. They identified outcomes for the lesson, planned instruction, and decided who would take the lead in the classroom for each section. They co-taught the lesson and planned a time to debrief.

When they met, Thompson and Escobar decided they had learned new things from working with one another. Escobar suggested that Thompson try co-teaching with the other 3rd-grade teachers to practice the new techniques. Thompson agreed and quickly went to work with her peers. Later, in Escobar's weekly summary to the staff, she invited Thompson to talk about the co-teaching experience and highlighted Thompson's work with the rest of the 3rd-grade team.

As she met for her weekly session with the principal, Escobar reflected on how the conflict between herself and Thompson pushed each of them forward in their practices. She also considered how her strategy to support Thompson was changing Thompson's perception of her role and responsibilities with the 3rd-grade team and students. Escobar was proud of how Thompson was assuming a leadership role.

The principal asked Escobar to reflect on how she handled the initial conflict resolution conversation with Thompson. The principal reinforced that Escobar showed courage and growth to address the conflict and take responsibility for her role in it. The principal then shared feedback about Escobar's interactions with other teachers, and Escobar set a goal of using some of the same strategies she found successful with the 3rd-grade team with the 5th-grade team and to report back at their next meeting.

Reflection questions

- How might you have responded as the coach in this situation? What reasons would you have for taking these actions?

- What might some reasons be for Thompson's resistance? How does understanding Thompson help Escobar choose strategies for working with Thompson?

- What might have contributed to the relationship dynamic between Escobar and Thompson?

- How did the principal contribute to or interfere with the situation? What is the principal's role in a situation like this?

- What guidelines might you suggest for coaches to handle similar situations?

Recommendations for

Central office administrators

- Provide professional development for coaches about partnership agreements with teachers.
- Share examples of communication brochures and handouts that coaches have created to explain coaching to teachers.
- Design a conflict resolution process to address any conflicts between teachers and coaches.
- Observe coaches carrying out their duties, and give them feedback on the partnership agreements they have created with teachers.

Building administrators

- Set clear expectations that coaches create partnership agreements with teachers.
- Define confidentiality between coaches and teachers in writing and refer to it often with teachers.
- Define the principal's and coach's roles in providing instructional leadership for the school.
- Communicate clearly to the staff expectations of how they will be involved with the school coach(es).
- Allocate time in teachers' workday to work with the coach to make interactions between coaches and teachers routine.
- Allocate a regular time to meet with the coach to monitor the impact of the work.
- Provide feedback regularly to the coach about coaching's effects.
- Help the coach communicate with the staff about what the coach is accomplishing.
- Ask the teacher to initiate the first contact to request to work with a coach.

Coaches

- Develop partnership agreements with teachers to define the work and clarify expectations of one another.
- Include the topic of confidentiality in the partnership agreements.
- Be receptive to feedback about coaching's impact, and adjust your behaviors based on the feedback.
- Create a means of communicating with teachers about available coaching services and work accomplished.
- Address conflicts with teachers or teacher teams as they arise.
- Seek opportunities and create structures to build teacher capacity. As often as possible, train another person in the building to coach.
- Co-facilitate teacher teams with grade-level and department heads.
- Ensure that teachers have a voice and choice about their work with the coach.

TOOL INDEX
Chapter 10

	TOOL	PURPOSE
10.1	**Sample coach rotation schedule**	Review this example of a coach's use of time during a typical week.
10.2	**Sample partnership agreement between coach and teacher**	Use this example to create an agreement between a coach and a teacher that defines their working relationship and expectations for the coach's work.
10.3	**Probing questions**	Try these sample questions while conducting a partnership conversation with a teacher.
10.4	**Staff survey**	Collect data on the needs of teachers at a site.
10.5	**Coach corner**	Understand a coach's weekly schedule and work accomplished.
10.6	**Feedback to coach**	Collect feedback about your performance as a coach.
10.7	**Protocol for problem resolution**	Try this process to manage conflict clearly and productively.

To download tools, see www.learningforward.org/publications/coachingmatters

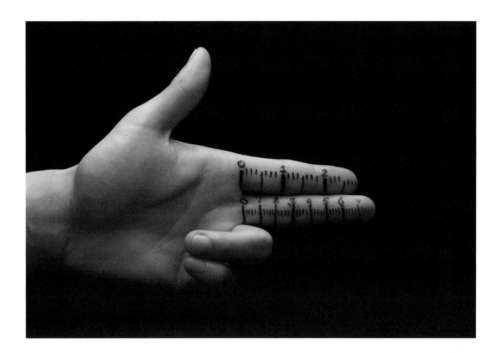

Evaluating
coaches and coaching

P art of creating and maintaining a coaching program is evaluating coaches' effectiveness and evaluating the program's effectiveness. After districts have invested in coaching, they also need to invest in evaluating how effective the coaching program and the coaches are. Evaluations yield data that can be used to plan, monitor, assess, and evaluate coaching's costs, processes, and effects.

Evaluation is often overlooked until several years after the program has begun or until someone needs solid evidence about the program's effects to weigh coaching against other improvement efforts vying for limited resources. The time to plan an evaluation of the coaching program and coaches is *before* the program is implemented — many crucial decisions are made during the planning phase that will affect the program evaluation.

All forms of evaluation give those in charge of coaching programs — and coaches — information to improve practices and results. Periodic, rigorous, scientific evaluations and informal feedback that emerge from conversations with teachers and principals help coaches improve their practices and increase results. Evaluation results are used to

An evaluation plan must be made public and the results of various assessments shared widely with all those affected by the program.

redesign and refocus the program for the future as evaluators learn what is working and what isn't.

The most effective evaluations include formative evaluation of the coaching program and of coaches that includes constructive feedback from multiple sources and a summative evaluation of the coaching program and of coaches based on specified criteria. A rigorous evaluation incorporates ongoing analysis of formative data and periodic summative data.

Coach supervisors, principals, and the district coaching steering committee, if there is one, are responsible for examining coaching's effectiveness. The steering committee also can communicate information about the program to all stakeholders (the steering committee is addressed in more detail in Chapter 2). An evaluation plan must be made public and the results of various assessments shared widely with all those affected by the program.

Evaluate the program

Begin the program design and evaluation by creating a theory of change. A program's theory of change specifies what the program does to produce its results. It guides operational decisions about the program and is the framework for the program's evaluation.

A theory of change and logic model

The theory of change is a map that helps define actions to be taken, the sequence for those actions, and the assumptions upon which the sequence is based. It details the program's structure, professional development available to coaches and their principals, ongoing support for coaches, how coaches organize their workday, and other program components (Killion, 2012). In addition to the program's theory of change, the program's logic model adds specificity by delineating how each action within the theory of change generates changes in the knowledge, attitudes, skills, aspirations, and behaviors needed to accomplish the defined goals (Killion, 2012).

The theory of change is based on a set of assumptions that explain the actions and action sequence within the theory of change. For example, the coaching program's goal is to improve student achievement, so core assumptions might include:

- Teachers are the most important factor influencing student achievement.
- Providing teachers support at the point closest to their interaction with students is the leverage point for increasing student achievement.
- Coaches focus on data-driven instruction aligned with standards for student learning.
- Coaches adapt their support of teachers to focus on curriculum, coherence, and consistency.
- Coaches use common conversation templates to provide support to teachers while adapting their work to meet teachers' individual and team needs.

These assumptions guide coaches, their principals, the teachers they serve, and the coach champion, who then are able to identify what changes are expected in teachers' knowledge, attitudes, skills, aspirations, and behaviors.

Program designers write a specific theory of change to explain how coaching is expected to lead to changes in teaching and student achievement. They then write specific goals and objectives.

Goals and objectives

When goals and objectives are clear, it is easier to design the program and evaluation and to outline the coaches' work. Designing the program with clear, measurable goals creates the framework for evaluating the coaching program. Goals answer the questions:

- What is the program intended to accomplish?
- What are its intended results?
- Whom will the coaching program affect?

Clearly defined goals include one or more student learning goals and goals for teacher practice written in SMART goal format (specific, measurable, attainable, results-based, and time-bound) or with goals and SMART objectives. The boxes below, Example 1 and Example 2, provide two models for how coaching program goals might look at the district, school, and classroom levels.

Example 1: Goals for coaching program		
LEVEL	**STUDENTS**	**TEACHERS**
Classroom	95% of students will improve their science performance by at least one level on the quarterly benchmark assessments in the next eight weeks.	100% of teachers will analyze student benchmark results and design instructional interventions to increase student science performance by at least one level on the quarterly benchmark assessments in the next quarter.
School	90% of students performing below proficient in science and math on the quarterly benchmark assessments will increase their performance by at least one level in the next quarter.	100% of teachers will implement data-driven instructional planning to narrow their focus of instruction in areas where students need the greatest attention in order to increase the performance of those students achieving below proficient on quarterly benchmark assessments.
District	90% of all students will perform at proficient or above on benchmark and end-of-year assessments in reading, math, and science by the end of the 2013-14 school year.	100% of the teachers will implement the district's instructional framework in their classrooms daily as measured by principal walk-throughs, peer walk-throughs, and principal observations.

Example 2: Evaluation goals and evidence

This example describes how a district, principal, and coach might evaluate the effectiveness of a coaching program.

The district establishes an overall learning goal for students:

• 95% of students will perform at the proficient level or above on the state end-of-year reading assessment in comprehension by the end of the 2012-13 school year.

The district specifies what evidence of success it will use:

• Evidence of success will be scores on the end-of-year reading assessment in reading comprehension.

The school has a school improvement goal:

• 100% of students scoring below proficient will increase their scores on the end-of-year assessment by at least 15% each year for the next two years.

The school specifies what evidence of success it will accept:

• Summative evidence: Scores on the end-of-year reading assessment in reading comprehension.

• Formative evidence: Scores on benchmark assessments; student classroom work samples.

The coach sets specific goals for changes in teaching that will achieve the district and school objectives, such as:

• Over the next two years, 100% of teachers will increase accuracy (achieving a score of 3 on a 4-point rubric) and frequency (daily) in applying identified reading comprehension strategies as measured by principal classroom walk-throughs and peer and coach visits.

The coach specifies acceptable evidence of success:

• Summative evidence: Mean scores on end-of-the-year principal walk-throughs and summative scores on teacher self-assessment of frequency of use.

• Formative evidence: Coach feedback to teachers using rubric; peer feedback using rubric; teacher monthly self-assessment of frequency of use.

Using the program's clear goals, the program designers determine what they hope to learn related to the goals — the basis of the evaluation. The questions to be answered may vary significantly depending on the audience. For example, school board members who want to know whether the district's investment in coaching is paying off have different questions from a coach who wants to consider how well the work with teachers is going.

Table 11.1 suggests some common questions about coaching that different audiences might have and evaluators may consider when designing the coaching program evaluation.

Table 11.1 Common coaching program evaluation questions by audience

AUDIENCE	QUESTIONS
School board	• Are students of teachers who participate in coaching achieving at higher levels? • What factors contribute to variances in coaching across the district? • Should we continue to invest in coaching? • Do teachers who have coaching support meet or exceed performance standards?
Coach champion	• What types of support most benefit coaches? • Is the coaching program being implemented with fidelity? • What coaching behaviors contribute to improved teaching and student learning? • What is effective about the coaching at an individual building? What are the coaching challenges at an individual building?
Principal	• Is the coaching program being implemented with fidelity to its design? • Do teachers benefit from coaching support? • Do students benefit when teachers have coaching support? • How are the school culture and teachers' willingness to collaborate changing as a result of coaching? • What support do coaches most need in order to be effective? • How does my support of the coaching program affect its success?
Coaches	• What effect does my support have on teachers, teaching, and student learning? • Is student achievement improving with coaching support? • Is teaching effectiveness greater with coaching support? • Am I differentiating support to meet individual and teaching team needs? • Do effects vary when I spend more time with individual teachers than with teaching teams? • How often do teachers follow through with the strategies we discuss? • How can I improve my support of teachers and increase their effectiveness and student achievement?

Evidence of effect

An effective evaluation is rigorous and ongoing. It uses multiple measures over time.

Every coach should establish goals that include clear and specific indicators of improvement in teachers' learning and practices (see Table 11.2). Principals and coaches may work together to write these goals using the SMART goal format and aligning the goals with school improvement plan goals intended to improve student achievement.

Progress on annual goals that lead to long-term desired outcomes needs to be measured so that the plan can be adjusted. One way to measure progress on annual goals is to use focus groups and questionnaires. Much of that information, however, is self-reported. Data from walk-throughs and observations can provide information about the level of use of coaching and the content of the coaching. Without knowing the program's level of implementation, it's impossible to measure coaching's effect on student learning.

Teachers, principals, and coaches themselves can contribute to the evidence. When teachers have the chance to evaluate how effective the

Establishing clear performance standards for coaches can help with decisions about coaches' daily work, principals' and colleagues' expectations, and coaches' ongoing professional learning and growth, as well as evaluation.

coaching they received is, they are more committed to the coaching program and share more about what kind of support is most helpful to them.

Students are another source of information. Survey students about teachers' instructional strategies or have a focus group conversation to collect perception data about the coaching program.

Effective assessment plans incorporate a variety of data collected from multiple sources affected by coaching and include teachers, students, principals, documents, and formal and informal assessment results.

Evaluate coaches

In some places, coaches are hired using funds from special programs such as a STEM initiative or Title I. As a result, the person overseeing STEM or Title I may be the coaching program's director. In other situations, the principal of the school

supervises the coach in that building. In districts where coaches work in multiple schools, principals give input on the coach's evaluation, but the central office staff member responsible for the coaching program is the coach's official evaluator. Regardless, clarity is essential about who formally supervises the coach program and coaches, as well as who provides input.

Coaches in most coaching programs face being evaluated using teacher standards. When coach evaluations use teacher standards, however, principals or other supervisors must extrapolate to apply those standards to coaching work, potentially making evaluations inconsistent. As the coaching program matures, principals and district human resources directors often realize that using teacher standards for coaches is inappropriate. Many districts have developed separate performance standards for coaches that befit their role. Jeffco (Jefferson County, Colo.) Public Schools uses a rubric to outline instructional coaches' expected knowledge, skills, attitudes, and action. Fairfax County (Va.) Public Schools has standards specifically for coaches.

Establishing clear performance standards for coaches can help with decisions about coaches' daily work, principals' and colleagues' expectations, and coaches' ongoing professional learning and growth, as well as evaluation. Clear standards also add validity to the coaches' performance evaluation by establishing fair, reliable, and reasonable performance expectations.

Coach evaluations should align with the district's approved educator effectiveness system and evaluation guidelines. Some districts that include student achievement as a component of teacher and principal evaluations are considering whether student achievement also should be part of a coach's evaluation. Several questions must be answered first:

- What is the coach's role in the district?
- How do coaches spend their time?
- How focused is coaching on instruction and student learning?

In practice, many coaches spend a considerable amount of time away from their core work because they are asked to take on unrelated tasks. If districts are going to measure the coach's success using student achievement, they must protect the coach's time to ensure that he or she is able to focus on instruction and related work.

Some districts give coaches opportunities for a coach champion to observe them each month and have a coaching conversation focused on the coach's work. Sometimes principals provide this support. In other districts, coaches take part in coaching labs where they periodically work with each other in order to sharpen and refine their practices. Ongoing observation and coaching of the coach help the coach refine his or her work.

Table 11.2 Sample coach goals, strategies, and portfolios

STUDENT ACHIEVEMENT GOALS from the school improvement plan	TEACHER PROFESSIONAL LEARNING GOALS	COACH STRATEGIES	EVIDENCE FOR PORTFOLIO
From fall to spring, increase student achievement on benchmark assessments in comprehension by 10% over last year's end-of-the-year scores.	Implement daily differentiated strategies to increase student comprehension.	Develop teachers' understanding and implementation of differentiated strategies for improving student comprehension through monthly whole school or team-specific professional learning.	• Schedule • Syllabi • Materials used • Teacher feedback on professional learning sessions
		Provide teams with weekly planning support to implement the strategies.	Log of planning sessions showing: • List of teachers attending • Topics discussed • Decisions made • Follow-up support requested

Table 11.2 Sample coach goals, strategies, and portfolios (cont'd)

STUDENT ACHIEVEMENT GOALS	TEACHER PROFESSIONAL LEARNING GOALS	COACH STRATEGIES	EVIDENCE FOR PORTFOLIO
		Model strategies in teachers' classrooms at their request.	Log showing: • List of requests for modeling • Date and time of model lesson • Date and time of debriefing • Summary of debriefing comments from teacher and coach • Schedule of coaching sessions • Focus of coaching session • Follow-up support requested • Compilation of staff survey on coach support • Student benchmark reading scores, specifically comprehension • End-of-year reading scores, specifically on comprehension
Increase by 15% the number of students scoring at the proficient level on the math end-of-the-year assessment.	Increase teacher use of formative assessments to determine student learning needs.	Develop teacher understanding of the purpose, design, and use of formative assessments.	• Schedule • Syllabi • Materials used • Teacher feedback on professional learning sessions
	Redesign instruction to address learning gaps.	Meet with teaching teams to design course-specific formative assessments for four units.	• Team meeting logs • Materials • Decisions • Follow-up requested • Formative assessments

Table 11.2 Sample coach goals, strategies, and portfolios (cont'd)

STUDENT ACHIEVEMENT GOALS	TEACHER PROFESSIONAL LEARNING GOALS	COACH STRATEGIES	EVIDENCE FOR PORTFOLIO
	Redesign student assignments to align more closely with standards.	Meet with teaching teams to interpret the results of formative assessments at the end of the four units. Plan the next instructional unit to address gaps. Include in the units student assignments that are focused more closely on math standards.	• Team meeting logs • Materials used • Decisions • Follow-up requested • Analysis of formative assessment data • New unit plans specifying ways to address gaps • Redesigned student assignments with indicators of the standards each assignment addresses written in student-friendly language
	Alter grading practices to give students more standards-focused feedback.	Revamp grading practices to include standards-based grading written in student-friendly language to share with students and parents, guidelines for specific feedback to include on student work, and rubrics written in student-friendly language to use for the four units during the school year.	• Standards-based grading plan • Feedback guidelines • Sample feedback given to students on assignments • Rubrics for four units • Compilation of staff surveys on coach support • Student benchmark and end-of-year scores, with percentage of students moving from below proficient to proficient and above

Use time log as reflection tool

Ask yourself:

- How does my work show that I am contributing to school improvement goals?

- Based on the data in my log, what example do I have that demonstrates that my work aligns closely with a team's or teacher's goals with whom I worked frequently? What data support the connection I am making?

- Based on these data, what might I change to align my work more closely with school, team, and individual goals for student achievement?

- What do these data tell me about my own goals for coaching? What would I consider a strength and an area for improvement?

- What factors contributed to the data? What circumstances helped or hindered my work during this period?

- What changes do I plan to make? What in the data tells me these changes are needed?

- What support will I want in order to make these changes?

Many coaching programs also ask coaches to report in a weekly or monthly log how they spend their time. Even if coaches are not required to submit time logs, they may track their own time in order to reflect on their work. Logs can offer supervisors and coaches valuable information to monitor and support coaches' work.

One instructional coach, for example, noted that he spent most of his time on areas related to students' reading performance, regardless of whether he was working with math, science, social studies, or language arts teachers. He talked with his principal about adding staff professional learning schoolwide on integrating pre- and post-reading strategies to push students to engage in more cognitively demanding tasks. This coach's review of his log helped him to see the pattern of requests for help with reading.

In addition to summative evaluations, coaches benefit from frequent and specific feedback from teachers and principals. Examining evidence in collaboration with teachers and principals is a good way for coaches to engage in continuous improvement.

Teacher feedback is an important feature of formative and summative assessments of a coach's effectiveness because teachers are a coach's primary clients. Teacher feedback can be anonymous and collected and compiled periodically during a school year. Coaches can get teacher feedback only as formative feedback or in their summative evaluation if stakeholders have developed clearly delineated agreements and parameters in advance about collecting and using feedback.

Teacher feedback can be collected in numerous ways, from using individual feedback forms after each interaction to using an overall feedback survey several times a year. Some methods are more appropriate for formative or summative evaluations of the coaching program, rather than for summative evaluation of the coach. For example, more qualitative feedback that often is more detailed and constructive helps in formative evaluations because these data might guide a coach to make immediate changes in practice. More quantitative feedback, such as the number of times a teacher worked with a coach, might be more useful in summative evaluations because it provides information over time.

Coaches also often ask for feedback in their individual and team conversations with teachers, especially through questions such as:

- Tell me how I can be more helpful in our next …

- What was most helpful to you in our time together today? What was least helpful?

- Given your learning preferences and goals, what do you want more of the next time we meet?

- There was a time today when you expressed confusion. Can you share with me how I might have contributed to that so that I can continue to grow as a coach?

Coaches can collect this informal feedback to reflect on and analyze their practices and to identify steps they need to take to become more effective. Coaches often miss opportunities to ask for in-the-moment feedback and hear teachers' perspectives on their work.

In addition to in-the-moment feedback from teachers, coaches can seek regular feedback from their principals and central office supervisors. Because these administrators have a different view of the coach's work and have specific expectations, they can offer important feedback. The coach might set up periodic meetings throughout a school year to focus specifically on formative feedback. These meetings may be part of a formal performance review or evaluation, but even if they are not, the coach still needs opportunities for formative feedback from supervisory personnel in addition to feedback from teachers.

When evaluators collect more formal feedback about the coaching program, coaches may be able to help supervisors and the coach champion analyze data from the surveys, interviews, or focus groups and use the data to think about ways to improve their own practices.

The more opportunities coaches have for formative feedback and support, the more quickly they will become master coaches with a laser focus on improving student learning.

Formative and summative evaluations

When coaches use formative and summative evidence to reflect on their effectiveness and results, they model for teachers the professional practice of frequently analyzing one's practice and ongoing learning. Formative and summative assessments of coaches' work help schools and districts support coaches' development and strengthen the coaching program.

Formative assessments include work samples, ongoing feedback from teachers and principals, individual and team reflections about the effectiveness of their practices, and student formative achievement data.

Summative assessment takes place within the coach's regular formal personnel evaluation and is aligned with the district's personnel evaluation policies and procedures.

Scenario

Marcos Garcia has been an instructional coach in his elementary school for four years. His large, urban district invested in supporting teachers by hiring a full-time instructional coach for every school and providing the coaches with extensive training to fill the roles of data coach, instructional specialist, learning facilitator and catalyst for change. The coaches, while housed in schools, are supervised by central office staff to support implementation of district curriculum initiatives.

As a coach, Garcia worked with almost all of the teachers in his building. Although some were more resistant than others, most were pleased with his support. Some experienced teachers, empathizing with new teachers' many challenges, gave up their coaching time so new teachers had more opportunities to work with Garcia.

When the district faced serious financial issues, some teachers in Garcia's school asked the teachers association to call for coaches to return to full-time classroom teaching. The teachers acknowledged that the coaches were gifted teachers and that their talents would benefit students. Association leaders also believed the coaches should serve students directly so the budget crisis didn't increase the student-teacher ratio. Some teachers in Garcia's school also told the association that they believed he could do more to improve student achievement by working directly with students in the classroom rather than supporting teachers. Association leaders then asked the district for evidence of the coaches' impact on classroom instruction and student learning.

In response, the district developed a coach evaluation rubric aligned with the program's defined outcomes. District leaders piloted and revised the instrument based on comments from coaches, coach evaluators, and school administrators. The district planned to use the rubric in the following school year after sharing it with teachers and coaches.

The association and district agreed to study the coaching program. The district hired an external consultant to evaluate the program, beginning with focus groups of all personnel who interacted with coaches. Leaders shared the focus group results with all district employees in an email in an effort to be transparent. They then implemented the focus groups' recommendations that had no budgetary implication and agreed to study recommendations that affected the budget. One major recommendation to be implemented was to ensure that all teachers had a choice in how to work with their coach.

Garcia, excited about giving teachers options for how to work with him, began a list of different supports he provided. He shared his list with the school staff and asked for additional ideas that he then compiled and posted on his coaching Web page. He also included the list on the back of his coaching request forms. Garcia was most excited that he would be able to work with teacher teams on lesson study, data dialogues, designing interventions, reviewing student work, and planning units while continuing to demonstrate lessons, co-teach, design differentiation, and conduct individual observations and conferences.

The district also implemented a recommendation to have coaches use a teacher survey to collect feedback on their practices. Garcia volunteered to serve on the committee to draft and pilot the survey prior to it being used districtwide the following school year.

As the district moved forward with its coaching program, Garcia realized that the district's deliberate efforts to evaluate and revise coaches' work gave him the information he needed to adjust his work each day and gave the district data to measure coaches' overall effectiveness as a lever for improving student learning.

Reflection questions

- What questions did the district's evaluation of the coaching program and coaches attempt to answer? What kind of questions would need to be included on a survey to answer them?

- What data are available in your school or district that would provide the kind of information that Garcia's association is asking for?

- How might Garcia have helped his colleagues understand how coaches support student achievement?

- What factors, besides the budget deficit, may be contributing to the teachers association's interest in evaluating the coaching program in this scenario?

- What are the advantages to having the district, association, and coaches agree to work together to design the evaluation survey? What are the potential problems in this arrangement?

Recommendations for

Central office administrators

- Plan and implement a coaching program evaluation to assess how well the program achieved its goals and provide annual data that can be used to continually improve the program. Evaluate the program every three to five years.
- Create evaluation instruments that align with the program's goals. Pilot and then revise the instruments so they provide relevant, useful, valid, and reliable information to use to continually improve the program.
- Set the expectation that coaches seek and use regular feedback (at least twice a year) from the teachers they serve. Support coaches in developing or accessing instruments for gathering teacher feedback. Have reflective conversations with coaches about what they are learning from the feedback.
- Expect coach champions to be on site for a significant amount of time so they may observe coaches and provide constructive feedback and support.
- Set the expectation that the coach champion will meet with the principal and coach several times each school year to review and document the coach's work.
- Establish criteria and procedures for evaluating coaches, and delineate the principal's and coach champion's roles related to coaches' evaluations.
- Establish and monitor an expectation that principals meet several times per year with coaches and coach champions to provide feedback to coaches about their work and to the coach champion about the coaching program.
- Create an exemplar of a coach's written evaluation.
- Evaluate the coach champion.

Building administrators

- Meet with your coach weekly to give feedback on his or her work and how it is affecting teachers and students.
- Provide simultaneous feedback to the coach and teacher.
- Meet with champions several times each year to review the fidelity of the program.

Recommendations for coaches

- Meet regularly with your principal for feedback.
- Seek and use teachers' feedback to improve your practice and to model how to ask for and use continual feedback.
- Study the program and coach evaluation rubrics or criteria to guide your actions.
- Approach conflict as a problem to solve, and seek a constructive, collaborative resolution.
- Align your work with district and school goals and with your own values.

TOOL INDEX
Chapter 11

	TOOL	PURPOSE
11.1	**SMART goals template**	Study the components of a SMART goal and use this form to plan one.
11.2	**Tools for measuring the impact of coaching on teaching and learning**	Read this outline of a variety of ways to measure the impact of the coaching program.
11.3	**Principal interview questions about the effectiveness of the coaching program**	Use questions such as these to collect feedback from principals about the effectiveness of the coaching program.
11.4	**Goal-setting template**	Use this template to set specific goals for a coach supporting a teacher's or team's efforts to increase student achievement.
11.5	**Focus group questions**	Use data from answers to focus group questions such as these for teachers, principals, and other coaches to revise your coaching program.
11.6	**Levels of Use framework**	Assess the level of implementation of a school initiative.
11.7	**Coach reflection template**	Keep a record of completed work and next steps for teams or individuals.

To download tools, see www.learningforward.org/publications/coachingmatters

Resource staff
as coaches

Budget reductions and reductions in support staff at the district and school levels have challenged those who value coaching as a support for teachers. At the same time, increased demands for personalized education are straining teachers' time. These conditions are creating new opportunities for schools to think about who coaches are and to become more creative about ways to provide teachers with access to coaching.

States, provinces, and school systems are recognizing current staff members' enormous expertise and tapping resource staff to become coaches, reallocating some or all of the work time of personnel whose roles have been focused on working with students or on managing school programs.

Literacy resources teachers who used to supplement student instruction now are serving teachers directly as subject-specific or general

> Some schools are using a tiered staffing model in which a master teacher leads a cluster of other teachers. In other districts, a coach works with mentor teachers who support one or more novice or new-to-school teachers in order to increase mentoring's consistency and effectiveness.

instructional coaches. School media specialists are providing additional services to teachers and expanding their responsibilities when a school may not be able to afford full-time library media services. Special education resource staff are becoming learning coaches to spread differentiated and inclusive instructional practices to all teachers. In other schools, department chairs or grade-level chairs are moving from managers to instructional specialists and working more directly with teachers on issues related to teaching and learning.

Some schools are using a tiered staffing model in which a master teacher leads a cluster of other teachers. In other districts, a coach works with mentor teachers who support one or more novice or new-to-school teachers in order to increase mentoring's consistency and effectiveness.

Principals have a key role in this shift. The principal's first role is recognizing the expertise within the schoolwide support staff. Not all resource staff will have the same level of expertise

in all areas. For example, the school's literacy resource teacher may model instructional practices within a classroom after providing schoolwide professional learning on the practices. The school's coach may then follow up with classroom visits to observe and give teachers feedback on how well they are using the new practices. While the coach is supporting teachers who are implementing the new practices, the literacy resource teacher may work with another group of teachers to develop curricular and instructional materials and also work directly with a small group of students who need supplemental instruction. This apparently seamless approach requires coordination, vision, and respect for each staff member's expertise.

Principals are responsible for coordinating resources to ensure that all resource staff are working toward common goals, spreading their services effectively and efficiently throughout the school, and scheduling so that their support is maximized and barriers to teachers' ability to implement new practices are minimal. Principals meet frequently with resource staff and coaches to coordinate and align focus, strategies, and audiences.

When schools maintain staffing levels and add coaching support, coordinated support from coaches and resource staff can maximize their effectiveness within the school.

Examples from the field

Districts and schools use a variety of strategies to add coaching services to support teaching and learning. When resource staff serve as coaches, the new coaches and teachers benefit — the coaches by gaining new skills and the teachers from increased classroom-specific support.

Media specialists

In the Fargo (N.D.) Public Schools, media specialists have had district training to become coaches and have found that their new knowledge and skills help them better collaborate with teachers. Teachers have traditionally viewed media specialists as information clearinghouses. Teachers asked the specialists for materials on a particular topic, and within a few days, resources appeared. Media specialists wanted to move past this role to partner with teachers as curriculum specialists and instructional specialists, as well as act as classroom supporters.

The Fargo media specialists continue to help teachers locate developmentally appropriate information and resources using subscription databases and the Internet, and they post website links on classroom resource pages. They help teachers design problem-based learning experiences and other inquiry-based performance tasks to create a more personalized, student-centered classroom where students use 21st-century skills. They work with teachers to co-create lessons that integrate information literacy, technology, and research from different disciplines into lessons and units. With the specialists' support, teachers have readily available resources that allow them to spend time on instruction rather than on finding, screening, and compiling classroom resources.

Fargo media specialists also work alongside classroom teachers to integrate technology into the classroom. Teachers often are anxious about managing technology, instruction, and students at the same time. Students sometimes are afraid to try a new approach to learning. With media specialists

serving as co-teachers in classrooms to support students with technology skills, teachers can focus on content learning. Working side by side with teachers, media specialists model the skills teachers need to integrate technology in the classroom and contribute to building teachers' confidence and capacity to act alone with technology.

Outside the classroom, media specialists collaborate with professional learning teams and demonstrate instructional strategies and technologies that support learning.

Media specialists in Fargo report that they feel more skillful and effective in their roles as media specialists and coaches because they have affected the quality of teaching. Having coaching skills gives them a deeper appreciation for

> With media specialists serving as co-teachers in classrooms to support students with technology skills, teachers can focus on content learning.

supporting teachers and developing interdependent, efficacious educators.

Special education resource teachers

In 2009, the Ministry of Education in Alberta, Canada, launched Setting the Direction, a comprehensive reform initiative to strengthen student success. One part of this initiative changes how teachers meet student needs, especially the needs of special education students, through instructional adaptations and modifications to help ensure continuous student learning growth. The premise in Alberta is that special education resource staff have specialized knowledge of instructional techniques for differentiating instruction and supporting inclusion of special education students in regular-education classrooms.

In this model, based on Response to Intervention, a learning coach collaborates with classroom teachers around Tier 1 and Tier 2 student interventions. The program defines a learning coach as "a fellow teacher acting as a mentor and

> As special education resource teachers transition from being direct service providers to coaching teachers, they have had to work with educators' mental models about the education of all students, particularly those with special needs.

facilitator to enhance the capacity for addressing diverse learning needs in the classroom" (Government of Alberta, 2009, p. 15). The learning coach's role is to build teacher and school capacity to support and respond to students' diverse learning needs.

As special education resource teachers transition from being direct service providers to coaching teachers, they have had to work with educators' mental models about the education of all students, particularly those with special needs. The transition also requires that those moving into the coach's role understand how teachers will respond to the changes and what support teachers will need in order to be successful. When coaches have this understanding, their interactions with colleagues will convey support and respect. The paradigm shifts are outlined in Table 12.1.

Other specialists

At Simonton Elementary School (Lawrenceville, Ga.), former Principal Dot Schoeller believed so strongly in the value of coaches that she transformed roles that typically served students through pullout programs into coaching positions. Literacy and math specialists became literacy and math coaches. English language learner and special education teachers became coaches.

The school, with 1,536 students, at one time had 20 coaches to support teachers in literacy, math, special education, and English language learning instruction, although it has fewer coaches today and almost 300 fewer students.

The coaches support classroom teachers, frequently co-teaching, sometimes with more than one coach in a classroom at a time (Richardson, 2008). To eliminate confusion or to make sure efforts were focused and not fragmented, Schoeller assigned coaches to serve specific grade levels. By serving particular grade levels, coaches developed trusting relationships with a group of teachers, were able to participate in daily common planning, and touched base with each teacher daily.

The investment in coaching paid dividends: the achievement gap closed and students in all population groups achieved at high levels, often outperforming schools in their large district that are far less diverse and serve fewer high-poverty students.

Teachers might have been pulled in multiple directions by 20 coaches. The principal's decision to assign coaches to specific grade levels and have frequent, principal-led meetings with all resource staff provided the coordination among the coaches needed to maintain the focus on the school's improvement goals. With more coaches

Table 12.1 Paradigm shift in specialist service model

FROM	TO
A discipline focus	An education focus
Discipline-specific goals and interventions	Discipline-specific only as necessary for the student to function effectively in the school and classroom
Assessment of special needs students for eligibility or funding	Assessment of students for educational programming
Interventions focused on changing the student	Interventions focused on changing the environment
Planning focused on the individual student	Schoolwide planning first, then planning for at-risk students, then planning for the individual student
Remediation of students already failing	Intervention for students at risk of failing
Assessment and diagnosis	Problem solving
Focus on individual differences	Focus on environmental and social variables
Emphasis on disabilities and deficits	Emphasis on strengths and what the student can do
Medically trained specialists	Educational specialists
Working independently	Working as part of a team
Providing services external to the school (for example, a clinic)	Providing services within the school
Direct intervention	Consultation and training others to intervene

Source: Mackenzie, N. (Ed.) (2009, April). *A review of the literature. Setting the Direction Minister's Forum*. Alberta, Canada: Alberta Education, p. 11.

available, Simonton teachers were better able to access services, and the teachers and coaches were able to find ways to reinforce students' core learning across disciplines.

Have a vision for the work

Those considering using resource specialists' expertise must decide how to allocate positions, time, and resources to support coaching. While decisions must be grounded in the school's and district's vision, leaders' desired outcomes, and school improvement goals, the first decision involves job descriptions. Some schools and districts have altered the specialists' current job description to allocate time for coaching.

Decisions must be made in several areas: Will specialists be released from some of their current responsibilities in order to serve as coaches, or will they be expected to embed coaching work within their current responsibilities? If the specialists are released from at least a portion of their

Resource specialists must examine their own mental models about how they effect change within their schools. Some believe that their current practices are the best way to meet student learning needs and that shifting their support to teachers creates a void.

work, how will their responsibilities be distributed or eliminated to allow time for coaching?

One way to have specialists coach is to help them learn coaching knowledge and skills and expect that they use coaching skills in their regular daily work as media specialists, special education providers, and so on. A coaching media

specialist, for example, might serve as a media specialist and use coaching skills within that role.

Another alternative is to rewrite the specialist's job description and require staff members to apply for the newly created position. Those interested have an opportunity to prepare and apply for a completely new role, and those who prefer to keep their original position can perhaps seek opportunities to remain in that position in a different school.

A third way is to divide the specialist's time, allowing the resource person to devote a portion of time to the resource role and another portion to coaching.

See the opportunities in challenges

Resource specialists have traditionally focused on working with students and may be uncomfortable at first with the shift in their role. They may have worked in their roles for years and be comfortable and have expertise in what they are doing. Many worry about how the students they served will continue to receive the personal support the specialists had provided.

Resource specialists must examine their own mental models about how they effect change within their schools. Some believe that their current practices are the best way to meet student learning needs and that shifting their support to teachers creates a void. Left unaddressed, these mental models will interfere with a school's or district's ability to transition resource staff from direct services to students to direct services to teachers.

With thought, the shift may be an opportunity for some to renew their roles, re-energize their work, and work collaboratively on professional learning and making decisions about instruction and student learning.

Teachers may worry about adding responsibilities if resource staff are no longer serving students. They also may worry about whether they will have the expertise to meet the needs of students previously served in pullout programs. Spending time discussing the benefits, assumptions, and perceived challenges of role shift can relieve some of the anxiety about the transition.

Parents, too, may worry when their children no longer receive specialized support outside the regular classroom. School and district leaders need to be ready to address these worries proactively, be sensitive to individuals' perceptions about the benefits and drawbacks of the change, and intervene quickly when problems occur.

The opportunities for improving teaching and learning expand when more educators are sharing knowledge and skill about teaching. As schools engage other resource personnel to add coaching expertise, teachers and students benefit. When the library media specialist coaches a teacher through open-ended questioning about how best to use a media resource with students,

the teacher's internal capacity to solve a problem and think critically about instructional decisions and resources grows. When special education resource personnel share their extensive knowledge and skills about teaching with all teachers rather than supporting a few students, all staff build their instructional expertise to differenti-

> The opportunities for improving teaching and learning expand when more educators are sharing knowledge and skills about teaching.

ate instruction. The expert strategies often used exclusively by special educators are used in classrooms with all students so more students experience effective teaching and fewer students need specialized education support. By spreading practices throughout a school so all teachers, rather than a few, use highly effective and adaptive teaching strategies, more students benefit.

Scenario

The principal and assistant principal meet with the instructional facilitators at Faraday High School every Tuesday. The instructional facilitators formerly were called department chairs, with the traditional duties assigned to that role. Their primary work had been managerial, with a focus on budgets, books, classroom assignments, and schedules. For the last two years, however, this team of teacher leaders led instruction across multiple disciplines and worked with clusters of teachers in small learning communities.

The leadership team developed a schoolwide focus on instructional practices in which all students were active learners, critical thinkers, readers, and writers. At the last Tuesday meeting, the assistant principal introduced several new instructional strategies to enhance students' critical thinking skills. Each instructional facilitator agreed to try at least one strategy in his classroom, co-teach using the strategy with another teacher, and bring back to the next meeting a few samples of student work representing all levels of student learning in the classroom.

By committing to learn the instructional processes first before they supported teachers in implementing the strategies, the facilitators gained a better perspective and appreciation for the work teachers would be asked to do. They also built good will with their peers, who recognized that the teacher leaders were risk takers and willing to practice what they were asking all teachers to do.

At the following week's meeting, the instructional facilitators looked together at the student work each had brought to understand how the strategies had affected student learning. They picked out a variety of examples of different levels of work to share with teachers when they presented the strategies later in the week.

The instructional facilitators next planned the presentation they would each do with small groups of teachers on the weekly late-start day later in the week. Because part of their responsibilities involved regular walk-throughs of teacher classrooms to provide feedback and support, they worked together to develop a list of actions they would be looking for as evidence that the strategies were being implemented. At the end of the meeting, they began to think ahead to the next month's focus — strategies to support procedural writing — led by the instructional facilitator who worked with the science and technology teachers.

The instructional facilitators began their planned work with their learning teams, helping teachers understand the instructional strategies, using the exemplars of student work they had selected, and sharing their own experiences with the strategies. They also shared the list of evidence of practice. The principal and assistant principal, too, met with small groups of teachers since they also served as instructional facilitators, taking on the same responsibilities the teacher leaders did.

Tight coordination among the instructional facilitators and school administrators helped send a common message to all staff about the schoolwide focus and increased teacher support for achieving the student results everyone wanted.

Reflection questions

- What significance does changing the department head title to instructional facilitator have? What message did the change send to staff?

- How did having the principal and assistant principal serving as instructional facilitators support or inhibit teacher commitment to implementing new instructional strategies?

- What were the advantages to the instructional facilitators first establishing a process for implementing the strategies in their own classrooms, examining how students responded, and identifying evidence of practice before sharing the strategies with teachers?

- How might instructional facilitators best identify topics to share with teachers? What advice would you offer about how to select or discover topics to improve student achievement?

- What do instructional facilitators need to know before giving teachers feedback on their use of new strategies? What partnership agreements would you recommend they establish with teachers before they give feedback?

Recommendations for

Central office administrators

- Consider resource staff members' talents and job skills and how those skills align with the expectations of coaches.
- Define the paradigm shifts staff need to make in order to transition from the role of resource provider to the role of coach.
- Examine the advantages and disadvantages of shifting resource staff to the coaching role or adding coaching responsibilities to their roles.
- Determine what current responsibilities resource staff will be required to continue in light of the change.
- Communicate to all staff the decision and rationale for shifting the roles and responsibilities of resource staff to include coaching.
- Screen existing resource staff members to ensure they have the knowledge and skills needed to succeed as coaches.
- Plan and provide training for resource staff on coaching skills.
- Plan and provide ongoing support and professional learning for resource personnel about coaches' roles and responsibilities.

Building administrators

- Clarify resource staff members' coaching roles and responsibilities.
- Establish clear guidelines for how resource staff will allocate their time among their varied roles.
- Provide the new coach with frequent feedback.
- Schedule a regular time for check-in conversations with the new coach.
- Ensure that all resource staff coordinate their services and work toward common goals.
- Ensure that resource staff provide services effectively and efficiently to all staff.
- Recognize each resource staff member's expertise, and match that individual's talents with teacher needs.

Coaches

- Work with other coaches and resource staff to meet the needs of all staff members.
- Match your area of expertise to teacher needs.
- Align services to individual, team, and schoolwide goals.
- Be ready to provide a clear and positive rationale for the transition in roles and responsibilities when asked.
- Seek support when needed from other coaches or the principal.
- Seek feedback from supervisors and teachers about their coaching services.
- Engage in ongoing professional learning to improve your practice.

TOOL INDEX

Chapter 12

	TOOL	PURPOSE
12.1	Sample action research project	See one district's approach to action research.
12.2	Library media specialist's partnership agreement with the principal	Review a media specialist's coaching agreement that helped strengthen her role.
12.3	Student support specialist job description and responsibilities	Use this sample job description to describe concrete coaching roles of student support specialists.
12.4	"Using a classroom-based coaching model to foster differentiation"	Read this article to explore how special education providers can provide professional learning support using coaching.

To download tools, see www.learningforward.org/publications/coachingmatters

Team
coaching

Changing teaching and student learning takes time, yet the speed of change can be accelerated when coaches work at least part of their day with teams of teachers rather than with individuals.

A team coach focuses on several teachers simultaneously and helps them to harness their power to help each other, according to Christine Thornton (2010).

The coach works with a group of members who share common learning goals, want to examine their own practice, and commit to developing transparency in their own and group members' practices.

Team coaching intends to move information into practice, just as one-on-one coaching does. Working one-on-one is a less efficient way, however, to make a substantive difference for teachers and students.

Coaches who work with teams of teachers give teachers the opportunity to engage with multiple thinking partners rather than one. Interactions are likely to be richer and deeper. Team members learn about their colleagues' strengths and explore how others think about teaching. They become

Team coaching artfully combines one-to-one and group coaching to provide the greatest potential for transforming practice in schools.

more interdependent. They build the capacity to support one another over time when the coach is not available, and so long-term change becomes more sustainable.

Team coaching is new to many in education. The idea emerged from the business practices of executive, or life, coaching and group facilitation and from the education practices of professional learning communities, critical friends groups, and learning teams.

Most educators come to team coaching with the expectation that it is group facilitation or a learning experience in which the coach teaches group members a concept, skill, or strategy. However, when team coaches help teachers learn processes to identify, solve, and reflect on challenges they face, coaches then can focus their efforts on the more complex aspects of teachers' learning, such as exploring their assumptions and beliefs and how they influence teachers' daily work. Coaches then are able then to support teams in new and different ways. Teachers learn skills that enable them to develop into teacher leaders themselves.

Team coaching is efficient and can be effective. It is not, however, a way to reduce the number of coaches needed. Team coaching artfully combines one-to-one and group coaching to

provide the greatest potential for transforming practice in schools.

Team coaching is specific, yet it shares some similarities with other common practices, such as professional learning communities, group facilitation, critical friends groups, or other forms of small group work. Table 13.1 lists the distinguishing characteristics of team coaching and other common group processes. These approaches are not mutually exclusive. Well-rounded systems of professional development and support embed all of these approaches in educators' daily work.

Team coaching benefits teachers

The benefits of team coaching include exponentially increasing the impact of coaching so that more teachers benefit from the coaching provided. In addition, team coaching supports group maturity, more rapid growth and development, innovation, teachers' confidence, and teacher capacity.

- **Group maturity.** Team coaching deepens the effects of teachers' collaborative learning. Coaches working with groups can use strategies to accelerate the team's maturation and increase the effects of collaborative work. The benefits of team coaching are evident when members are able to sustain their relationships over time, develop genuine trust for one another, and become willing to step out of their own comfort zones. Most teams in schools never reach this point of maturation without coaching.

- **More rapid growth and development.** With team coaching, group members commit to their own growth and that of other members. Individual members feel supported by the group and that they are not alone in facing the challenges or striving for the goals they seek to reach. That sense of support often enhances their willingness to step out of

Table 13.1 A comparison of group learning approaches

	TEAM COACHING	**PROFESSIONAL LEARNING COMMUNITIES**	**GROUP FACILITATION**	**CRITICAL FRIENDS GROUPS**
Characteristics	Membership remains stable over a period of time.	Membership may remain constant or may vary.	Membership is usually determined by the task to be completed.	Membership may remain constant or vary. Membership sometimes is determined by the protocol or the presenter's goal.
Membership	Members may or may not be an intact team sharing the same students, goals, curriculum, and so on. Group members benefit from varied perspectives.	Members most often are an intact team sharing a common curriculum, students, goals, needs, and so on.	Members may or may not be an intact team. Members' skills or insights are needed to accomplish a particular task or goal, such as solving a problem, or developing a product or process.	Members most often are an intact team sharing common curriculum, students, goals, needs, and so on. Some groups include a more diverse membership.
Team size	3 to 8	3 to 10	Team size varies by the work to be done and can be quite large, such as a task force or leadership team.	6 to 10
Member expectations	To improve individual and team member practices and results and to contribute to team members' well-being.	To engage in the cycle of continuous improvement and share responsibility for achieving common student achievement goals and educator learning goals.	To contribute to attaining a goal.	To reflect on one's own and peers' work. To critique peers to improve the peers' work.

Table 13.1 A comparison of group learning approaches (cont'd)

	TEAM COACHING	PROFESSIONAL LEARNING COMMUNITIES	GROUP FACILITATION	CRITICAL FRIENDS GROUPS
Facilitator	Facilitated by a skillful coach who is not a member of the team and who understands coaching processes and how to build trust, manage conflict, and maintain the standards of effective teamwork.	May or may not be facilitated. Facilitator may be external to the group or a group member. Facilitator is skillful, understands the cycle of continuous improvement, and knows basic group processes.	May or may not be facilitated. Facilitator may be external to the group or a group member. Facilitator is skillful, understands the cycle of continuous improvement, and knows basic group processes.	Uses a trained facilitator who adheres to protocols and maintains the standards of effective teamwork.
Processes used	A range of coaching processes that meet the goals of the team or individual member in the spotlight to improve practice and results.	A defined process based on the cycle of continuous improvement that includes analyzing data, setting goals, learning strategies, reflecting on implementation, and evaluating progress.	Varied processes specific to the desired outcome.	Standard protocols selected based on the goal.
Results achieved	Individual and common team goals often related to improving professional practice and student achievement.	Common team goals often related to improving professional practice and student achievement.	Common team goals often related to improving professional practice and student achievement.	Common team goals often related to improving professional practice and student achievement.

Table 13.1 A comparison of group learning approaches (cont'd)

	TEAM COACHING	PROFESSIONAL LEARNING COMMUNITIES	GROUP FACILITATION	CRITICAL FRIENDS GROUPS
Length of time	Often a defined period of time or set number of meetings spanning several months or longer.	Ongoing.	Determined by the amount of time required to accomplish the task or goal.	Often a school year or longer.

their comfort zone. The nonevaluative nature of interactions within team coaching provides teachers with a safe place to take risks.

- **Innovation.** Team coaching often supports more inquiry and innovation because multiple perspectives are represented. In one-to-one coaching, the teacher has only the coach's perspective. Bringing multiple perspectives to the coaching situation expands the possibilities beyond what the coach and teacher can imagine. Synergy emerges when teachers with diverse ideas interact.

- **Teachers' confidence.** Learning a new skill is macro-level learning that often occurs in more formal professional learning such as a workshop. However, that learning does not become useful or valuable until it is transferred into practice. Team coaching creates opportunities for team members to share their experiences, compare them, and examine the practice from multiple perspectives, enriching each individual's understanding. Through this feedback, teachers are supported in transferring macro-level learning to micro-level learning (Curry & Killion, 2009).

- **Teacher capacity.** Finally, team coaching builds capacity of team members to understand the dynamics of coaching so that they can use some

of the processes independently or as a team without the coach.

Team coaching has pitfalls

Team coaching has several potential pitfalls: inefficiency, groupthink, competition, ineffectiveness, and time. Most of these occur when the coach is not prepared to coach a team or when members have inaccurate assumptions or expectations about team coaching.

- **Inefficiency.** Some will expect the coach to tell them what to do in particular situations. Team coaching, rather than being directive, is organic. The goals, outcomes, and results emerge from the individuals within the team through the consensus of the team. Most teachers are familiar with training as another experience in which they work collaboratively with others, so they will find significant differences between team coaching and training in which their learning is shaped by a learning facilitator. As a result, they may be frustrated when they come to team coaching, expecting the coach to direct the coaching session but finding that there is little direction.

- **Groupthink.** Team members begin to agree so frequently or to develop such strong relationships that they fail to think critically about one another's ideas or to challenge each

Despite the many obstacles to team coaching, the benefits abound. Skillful facilitation and coaching will help coaches and teams avoid pitfalls or resolve the issue.

other's assumptions and beliefs. Groupthink may also occur within groups that are uncomfortable with or unprepared to handle conflict within the group, so members choose to agree with one another to preserve harmony rather than question or surface ideas with which others may not agree. As a result, team coaching sessions may not move members cognitively, attitudinally, or emotionally.

- **Competition.** Team coaching begins with a group that shares a common goal — from a group that wants to help an individual member achieve his or her own goal to a group working to achieve schoolwide improvement. When teams lack a common goal and team members compete to make their own goals the priority, team coaching can become competitive. Effective team coaching depends on group members collaborating and agreeing on a shared focus and purpose.
- **Ineffectiveness.** Another obstacle in team coaching is the level of commitment and teacher engagement. For team coaching to succeed, all participants should commit to active and authentic engagement. When any one pulls back or opts out, it affects the entire team's success. When someone opts out of engaging in a team coaching session, this is a team challenge, not an individual one. All team members share

responsibility for whatever is creating the hesitation. Acknowledging responsibility and acting on it is difficult for many teachers who prefer that others handle difficult situations.

- **Time.** Another challenge to team coaching is finding time. Team coaching cannot be completed in a 20- to 30-minute meeting. It requires focus and commitment. Teachers often feel pressured by their multiple responsibilities and are unable to allow themselves to engage in a team coaching session. They may even see it as selfish. Yet focusing on renewal and growth is one positive way to meet the many responsibilities and to meet them with expertise gained from team coaching.

Despite the many obstacles to team coaching, the benefits abound. Skillful facilitation and coaching will help coaches and teams avoid pitfalls or resolve the issue.

Lay solid groundwork

Successfully coaching a team requires laying some groundwork. One of the most important steps of team coaching is creating a clear partnership agreement that defines with specificity the team's purpose, the individual and team goal(s), and the coach's role.

In team coaching, the agreement is between the coach and the team and is also among team members. Partnership agreements:

- Establish explicit individual and team goals and indicators that will measure progress toward those goals.
- Make explicit the coach's and team members' expectations.
- State team norms or expectations that address safety, confidentiality, language, participation, time, processes, and commitment.

- Provide protocols or processes that create a sense of safety for all members.
- Set up debriefings of the experience to improve members' engagement and the coach's actions.
- Provide for a meeting place that makes all members feel safe and comfortable.

Team coaches also may want an agreement allowing them to use team coaching to develop individual and team communication and collaboration skills. By making team members more aware of particular examples of communication and collaboration skills, the coach can, with the group's permission, help team members analyze the connection between a behavior and response.

Team coaching uses various approaches to achieving individual and team goals. Groups such as the Coalition of Essential Schools and National School Reform Faculty have developed and tested protocols that are helpful in team coaching. Team coaches also may vary some strategies used in one-on-one coaching. Other useful strategies have their roots in group counseling. The strategies included in the tools for this chapter describe processes to reach individual and team goals and are for coaches with any level of experience who want to team coach.

Two basic forms of team coaching are called one-in-some and all-for-one. In the first approach, the team contributes to one team member's goal while members keep their individual and team goals private. The scenario in this chapter is an example of this form of team coaching. The second form of team coaching is all-for-one, in which team members share a common goal and work with the coach to achieve it. The focus of the shared goal may be to solve a problem, develop a product, inquire, learn, become more self-aware, assess, or another goal-focused action. For example, when teachers decide that they want to try a new strategy to help students learn to organize ideas in written text, their common goal is to improve student content-area writing. The tools that supplement this chapter indicate which form of team coaching is most appropriate for which approach.

Figure 1 Types of coaching

One-in-some coaching

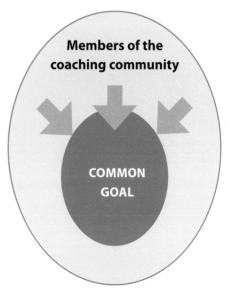

All-for-one coaching

Scenario

As an experienced coach, Sherida Franklin recognized that teams of teachers working together often accomplish more and develop a stronger sense of community. Franklin suggested to her principal that they change the expectation about how she used her time. She wanted to increase her time with teams and spend less time with individuals.

As the two looked at the schedule for teachers' common times, it was apparent that the greatest struggle would be to find time for Franklin to meet with the teams. Coaching individuals, Franklin could meet with a teacher at most times during the day, either while the teacher was in class or during the planning period. The flexibility was greater than with teams, many of which met during the same common planning times. However, the principal understood and valued Franklin's interest in supporting teacher teams, so she worked to revamp the schedule midyear to provide more varied times for teacher teams to meet.

The math team had an established meeting every second and fourth Monday, so Franklin began with this group. Getting this team to understand what the group might accomplish together took time, however, because the teachers immediately wanted to write curriculum and lesson plans. Franklin explained that team coaching helps individuals and teams identify issues to resolve and goals to work toward.

As she explained, a new math teacher, Martin Wu, shared that he was frustrated by students who wanted one right answer to a math problem. Wu wanted to give up on the math curriculum that emphasized concepts, thinking out loud, explaining, and divergent processes. Franklin invited Wu to consider a one-in-some team coaching session.

At the coaching session, Wu set a goal of identifying specific strategies he could implement immediately to help students understand the value of multiple strategies for approaching math. The team's goal was to help Wu feel less alone in this common challenge, to help him stay open to possibilities, and to create a list of at least 12 viable strategies he could use with his students.

Franklin asked Wu to describe the situation to the team and how it made him feel. She next asked him to describe what he wanted and what success would look like. Wu explained his ideal class: one in which students embraced explaining their thinking, were comfortable with multiple processes, and were able to understand multiple results.

Franklin asked team members to describe what success might look like in order to expand Wu's vision of what was possible. She next asked team members to share ideas for reaching that ideal. With each idea offered, she asked the team member to explain how the idea might work in practice and why it might work, and she encouraged teachers to link their explanations to a specific principle related to math pedagogy. Franklin also reminded teachers to speak in possibilities using might or may rather than declarative statements or absolutes. She asked Wu to record each idea offered.

Toward the end of the meeting, when Franklin asked Wu to recap the list of suggestions, he had noted 17 ideas. She asked him to name a few that stood out for him and to share why those ideas seemed notable. She then asked team members which ideas jumped out for them and to explain their thinking. Finally, Franklin asked Wu and team members to comment on whether they had reached their goals for the coaching session.

Note: Because team coaching takes many forms, it is difficult to use a single scenario to illustrate its value.

Reflection questions

- What are the potential side effects, both positive and negative, of team coaching? What can coaches do to maximize the positive ones and minimize the negative ones?

- What factors do you consider in order to determine whether team coaching is preferable to individual coaching? What indicators would suggest that team coaching might be inappropriate?

- The team-coaching scenario describes a process that Franklin used to engage all members of the team. What aspects of the process might have contributed to Wu's willingness to share his challenges and feelings with colleagues?

- Team coaching requires a tremendous amount of trust among the members of the team, yet it might also be the very strategy that can build trust. Given that it both requires and builds trust, how do coaches know when enough trust is in place to support team coaching?

- Given the characteristics of the culture within your school or district, what elements might need to be included in the partnership agreements between coaches and principals and between coaches and team members to support the effective use of team coaching?

Central office administrators

- Review the definition and goals of coaching to determine whether team coaching is consistent with what exists or if changes are needed. If changes are needed, create a timeline for making those changes.
- Determine what percentage of a coach's time is devoted to individual and team coaching and how to monitor this expectation.
- Create the expectation and a support system to make time available for team coaching within the workday so all teachers have equal access to team coaching opportunities.
- Establish a system of professional learning that provides multiple vehicles of support for strengthening teaching and student learning, with team coaching as one vehicle.
- Provide professional learning for coaches on how to coach teams.
- Provide teachers and coaches with professional learning on collaboration and team process skills so coaches and teachers are more adept at interacting.
- Have coach champions offer coaches feedback on their effectiveness with teams in order to refine coaches' skills.
- Engage coaches in team coaching to extend and refine their team coaching skills.

Building administrators

- Establish a schedule that allows teachers to participate in team coaching.
- Create a coaching infrastructure so that teachers participate in individual coaching and team coaching within a system of professional learning.
- Provide coaches with feedback on team coaching to demonstrate support.
- Participate in team coaching sessions.
- Coach a team.
- Set clear expectations for teachers that they participate in team and individual coaching.
- Ensure that the coaching program's goals align with individual, team, school, and district goals for improvement.

Coaches

- Set a schedule that includes coaching teams and individuals.
- Seek feedback from team members, coach champions, and your administrator on techniques for coaching teams.
- Participate in team coaching to strengthen individual practice.
- Develop skills in multiple approaches to coaching teams.

TOOL INDEX
Chapter 13

	TOOL	PURPOSE
13.1	**Help groups**	Use this protocol when a team wants to support an individual member facing a challenge.
13.2	**Here's the situation**	Try this tool as an alternative protocol for teams wanting to support one member addressing an issue, putting themselves in that colleague's shoes.
13.3	**Metaphors**	Gain guidance as a coach by encouraging team members to explore and share pressing issues through divergent thinking and the use of the familiar to understand the unfamiliar.
13.4	**Questions to consider**	As a coach, help a team member expand his or her perspective on a situation that causes dissonance.
13.5	**Principles we live by**	Learn as a coach to help team members identify principles and assumptions associated with various issues, topics, or problems.

To download tools, see www.learningforward.org/publications/coachingmatters

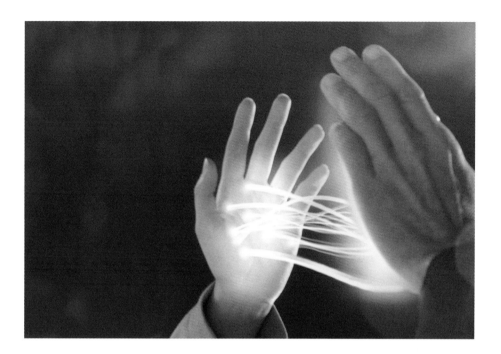

The future
of coaching

Experts may disagree about the value of class size, the number of students in a school, or what constitutes adequate funding, but researchers agree that the quality of teaching has the largest effect on student learning (Institute for Educational Leadership, 2001, p. 1). Coaching will continue to be useful in improving teaching — and student achievement. With nearly every school in the nation facing significant changes from implementing new college- and career-ready standards, more rigorous assessments, and as-yet-unknown initiatives, teachers will need more coaching rather than less.

Those discussing the future of coaching acknowledge coaching's power to improve teaching and learning and to create a collaborative learning culture. Coaching will evolve just as teaching and learning are evolving. Coaches will build new capacity for school leadership, continue to influence individual teachers and teacher teams, build organizational capacity, and adapt with technology.

Coaches build capacity

Coaches are driven to improve learning for all students and play a central role in ensuring quality teaching for every student. They are, in short, teacher leaders.

Jennifer York-Barr and Karen Duke define teacher leadership as "the process by which teachers, individually or collectively, influence their colleagues, principals, and other members of the school communities to improve teaching and learning practices with the aim of increased student learning and achievement. Such teacher leadership work involves three intentional development foci: individual development, collaboration or team development, and organizational development" (2004, pp. 287–288).

Improvements in student learning will occur

through school-focused professional learning led

by teachers for teachers.

York-Barr and Duke's three intentional foci align with findings in *Professional Learning in the Learning Profession: A Status Report on Teacher Development in the United States and Abroad*, which yielded a number of considerations for improving teachers' practice and student learning: "[M]any schools and districts across the country have invested in school-based coaching programs, one of the fastest growing forms of professional development today. Typically in such models, administrators identify well-regarded veteran educators and assign them to provide ongoing guidance, advice, and mentoring to a group or groups of teachers to help them improve their instruction" (Darling-Hammond et al., 2009, p. 11).

In their comparison of U.S. schools to other countries whose students outperform U.S. students, Darling-Hammond et al. conclude, "While American teachers participate in workshops and short-term professional development at similar levels as teachers in Organisation for Economic Co-operation and Development nations, the United States is far behind in several respects. The nation lags in providing public school teachers with chances to participate in extended learning opportunities and productive collaborative communities in which they conduct research on education-related topics; to work together on issues of instruction; to learn from one another through mentoring or peer coaching; and collectively to guide curriculum, assessment, and professional learning decisions" (p. 27).

Improvements in student learning will occur through school-focused professional learning led by teachers for teachers. In some schools, coaches are formally designated; in other situations, teachers step into the coach role without the formal designation. Other times, coaches will be members of a learning team with a shared commitment to improvement. Within such communities of practice, leadership may change as different members step up to facilitate. In other cases, the community will be leaderless, and every member will share equally in the responsibility of supporting colleagues' learning and professional growth. In the case of communities of practice with a facilitator, the facilitator assumes the lead learner or coach responsibilities. In the case where the community is leaderless, every member is a coach of other members.

When school staff commit to learning and growing together, research confirms that their joint learning has a greater effect on student learning. According to Darling-Hammond and her co-authors (2009), teachers benefit and students show significant gains in achievement when teacher professional learning is sustained and intensive. Teachers typically need close to 50 hours of learning in a given area to improve their skills and their students' learning.

Teachers say that their top priorities for further professional learning are learning more about the content they teach (23%), classroom management (18%), teaching students with special needs (15%), and using technology in the classroom (14%) (Darling-Hammond et al., 2009).

Teachers are not getting adequate training in teaching special education or limited English proficiency (LEP) students. More than two-thirds of teachers nationally had not had even one day of training in ways to support the learning of special education or LEP students in the previous three years, and only one-third agreed they had been given the support they needed to teach students with special needs.

American teachers spend much more time teaching students and have significantly less time to plan and learn together, or to develop high-quality curriculum and instruction, than teachers in other nations. U.S. teachers spend about 80% of their total working time engaged in classroom instruction, compared with about 60% for other nations' teachers who have more time for joint planning and collaborative professional learning, as well as to develop curriculum and instruction.

Coaches address these findings every day in their work. They maximize the effects of professional learning by linking it directly with what teachers do each day in their classrooms, exponentially expanding opportunities for teacher learning and focusing attention on the content, students, and environment in which teachers teach. They do this by making professional learning the everyday

action of teachers. They do it also by being skillful facilitators of professional learning who know and use Learning Forward's Standards for Professional Learning (see p. 87) to guide their practice and who develop others' expertise to be advocates for effective professional learning.

Coaches influence individual teachers

A single coach in a school or even a few coaches in a district cannot provide the intensive, ongoing, job-embedded professional learning and class-

Stand-alone professional development will be replaced with ongoing, job-embedded learning that is part of the teacher's daily work.

room support needed to realize the goal of having every student achieve at level.

Learning will increasingly move from individual teachers working in isolation to teachers working collaboratively in teams. Stand-alone professional development will be replaced with ongoing, job-embedded learning that is part of the teacher's daily work.

Coaches will help shift the school culture from one of accountability, one in which educators are forced into change, to a culture of responsibility, one in which educators adopt changes because it is the right thing to do for students. Coaches will support transformational learning and develop teachers' problem-solving skills for adaptive work rather than focusing only on transmitting information and providing technical assistance, as often happens now.

Coaches will study evolving research about the brain and learning to develop greater expertise about how students learn. They will be able to help teachers bridge the knowing-doing gap by supporting them as they deepen their understanding. Rather than mechanistically following a teacher's guide, then, teachers will be able to make instructional decisions based on a scientific rationale and communicate that rationale. When teachers can define research- and evidence-based reasons for their instruction, they can better improve and sustain student learning.

Cultures of inquiry grow when coaches help other teachers acquire and use facilitation skills.

Coaches will support classroom teachers through co-planning, co-teaching, modeling, and observing with feedback. More students today have different learning preferences, academic preparation and abilities, personal habits, and physical and behavioral attributes. Effective coaches will tap into their own and others' content expertise and specialized understanding of teaching students with disabilities to support quality instruction in every classroom for every student.

Coaches will link their work directly to specific student learning goals and school and district improvement goals. The ongoing support that coaches provide will be key to school improvement and school reform efforts.

Coaches influence teams

Coaches are culture builders. Coaches who work closely with teachers and their students each day are best suited to recognize the specific instructional refinements teachers need and to work with them to implement these refinements, because coaches have a trusted, professional respectful relationship with their colleagues. They are on site, able to work alongside teachers in the classroom every day. They can provide sustained, job-embedded professional learning among teams of teachers focused on content-specific and student-specific learning needs.

They build a culture of inquiry based on trust and their strong relationships. Cultures of inquiry are grounded in shared assumptions and beliefs that every voice counts, that working together problems can be solved, and that no person has the entire truth. Coaches support development of these skills and attitudes through modeling, training, and coaching teachers in using these skills and attitudes.

In a culture of inquiry, all staff, not just a few, benefit when they understand the change process, reasons for resistance, stages of community development, and strategies to move teams forward while remaining focused on their goals.

Cultures of inquiry grow when coaches help other teachers acquire and use facilitation skills. Coaches model and develop others' skills by facilitating teams in working to improve teaching and student learning and by serving on leadership teams with other teacher leaders who collaborate with the principal to influence the school's direction and decisions and carry out the plan to achieve the school's vision. Coaches model for others how a single person can work within teams to shape the destiny of a school, its staff, and its students.

As coaches strive to improve the quality of teaching, they are simultaneously building a cadre of teacher leaders and future coaches. Every teacher ideally will develop the capability to serve as a coach. As coaches support others' teaching, they develop an increased acuity about what makes effective practice. When all teachers develop this expertise through continuous professional learning and reflective practice, every student in a school benefits.

Coaches who commit to developing coaching expertise in their peers can lead teachers to develop the skills and attitudes needed to transform school cultures.

Coaches build organizational capacity

In the United States, teachers have limited influence on crucial areas of school decision making. Less than one-fourth of teachers feel they have great influence over decisions and policies (Darling-Hammond et al., 2009). Teachers in many high-achieving nations, on the other hand, have substantial influence on school-based decisions, especially curriculum and assessment development and the design of their own professional learning.

Fred Newmann and Gary Wehlage (1995) propose, "(If) schools want to enhance their organizational capacity to boost student learning, they should work on building a professional learning community that is characterized by a shared purpose, collaborative activity, and a collective responsibility among staff" (p. 37).

When teachers engage in team-based collaboration, teaching gaps are more readily addressed. Coaches provide support for teachers to engage in routine learning walks or other forms of learning with their teams, giving teachers opportunities to define aspects of quality instruction and further develop their expertise in teaching.

A coach who is a skilled facilitator helps teachers take responsibility for adding their voices to dialogue and discussions about school-based decisions, especially those related to their professional learning around curriculum, assessment, and instruction. Coaches can train teacher leaders in facilitation skills so the school has more resources to create effective professional learning teams in which teachers use structures, tools, and strategies to build trust and cultures of inquiry.

As more public schools in the United States recognize and respond to the needs of novice teachers, teacher induction programs may be folded into collaborative communities of practice, enabling novice and experienced teachers to coexist and learn with and from one another, and enabling coaches to provide ongoing support to develop teachers' skills throughout their careers.

Gutierrez and Bryan (2010) found that teachers began to identify themselves as teacher lead-

> Coaches provide support for teachers to engage in routine learning walks or other forms of learning with their teams, giving teachers opportunities to define aspects of quality instruction and further develop their expertise in teaching.

ers after an online learning experience facilitated by an instructional coach, learning about 10 roles of coaches (Killion & Harrison, 2006), regular opportunities to reflect on their role as leaders, and opportunities to engage with other teachers about their experiences supervising student teachers.

In these ways, then, coaches will help to expand teacher leadership.

Coaches adapt with technology

Technology is reshaping professional learning and coaching to change teaching. Online support may never fully replace the face-to-face coaching many teachers experience, but technology will become increasingly important and helpful in teacher professional learning. As a result, teachers will need to become more competent with using technology. Virtual coaching gives teachers access anywhere, any time — even after hours. Bud-in-the-ear coaching allows teachers to get instantaneous feedback from a coach observing in the classroom.

In China, some teachers-in-training link with their university advisers via webcam. In some places in the United States, teachers wear transmitters in their ears linked to walkie-talkies that coaches use to offer just-in-time recommendations to adjust teaching practice. In global communities of practice, Web-based networks

> Social networking may become a common tool for coaches and teacher leaders.

of educators exchange resources, link their classrooms, and share student work. Students share learning products with fellow students around the world while teachers compare notes on teaching core concepts. Nearly every teacher, no matter the nation, has access to limitless, free resources for teaching and learning.

Coaches will find it less important over time to bring resources to teachers as districts create or link to instructional support systems that bring resources into a central archive and make them readily available to teachers. Instead, coaches will focus their efforts on helping teachers use these systems, diagnose and assess student learning, and align their efforts with curriculum standards to personalize students' learning. And just as they want teachers to personalize student learning, coaches, too, will tailor their support to educators' individual and team needs. Coaches will find instructional support systems designed to help them coordinate and facilitate teacher learning.

Social networking may become a common tool for coaches and teacher leaders. Social networking can support teacher leaders' growth and development by providing access to information, engaging them in problem solving and inquiry, helping them share perspectives, and providing just-in-time support. Online communities allow coaches and teacher leaders to connect with and support each other and to expand communities' collective wisdom. These communities are most beneficial when they support and strengthen teachers' local, face-to-face communities.

Gutierrez and Bryan (2010) found that providing focused, weekly online professional learning for student-teacher supervisors resulted in rich discussions, peer support, and timely feedback. Teachers' needs were met in real time as they occurred, and they gained confidence as mentors and belief in themselves as teacher leaders.

The future of coaching

Educators serving in leadership roles, particularly principals and coaches, must adapt to a rapidly changing environment. The current organizational structures under which schools operate will need to be reimagined. In our rapidly changing world, the vision for coaching must also respond to new and unknown needs.

Shifting budgetary priorities are making it increasingly challenging for district and school leaders to find the resources to fund coaching positions. Rather than abandon coaching as an appropriate intervention for supporting teaching and learning, it is important to examine alternatives to current coaching practices and continue to provide coaching support, although perhaps in different ways.

The current model of one coach per school may no longer be financially feasible or even

Questions for leaders

Leaders who work closely with coaches need the skills to adapt to quickly changing schools and communities. Leaders will want to consider:

- What knowledge and skills do coaches need in order to be able to affect teaching and learning?

- How can coaches help teachers connect neuroscience with student instructional needs?

- How can coaches help teachers become globally knowledgeable?

- How will coaches help teachers align curriculum, instruction, and assessment to prepare students to be citizens in a global society?

- How will leaders and coaches address factors of school culture that contribute to, as well as threaten, teacher leaders' development?

- How do leaders and coaches create the type of culture that supports teacher leadership development?

- How might leaders and coaches apply Killion and Harrison's coaching framework (2006) to develop building-level professional learning for classroom teachers?

- What professional learning will help develop a school culture in which teachers take a stance of inquiry and take on leadership roles?

- How might the roles of noninstructional support personnel, such as special education providers, psychologists, and social workers, be reimagined in order to build teachers' knowledge?

- What are the special challenges in different kinds of schools, such as rural, small, large, urban?

practical with the opportunities available through technology. A single coach or even a team of coaches in a school is unlikely to meet all teachers' needs effectively. The definition of coaching — improving the quality of instruction and increasing student learning — means coaches may never work themselves out of a job; however, they will also never meet the complex and increasing needs of their colleagues as they had hoped.

These circumstances may require that how teachers receive coaching changes. The very act of coaching may take on a new look. Who serves as coaches may be different in the near future.

Perhaps the future will embrace the vision of every teacher being a coach rather than only a few teachers as coaches to promote the idea that continuous improvement is the primary responsibility of every professional educator. Technology also may change how coaching is provided. Regardless of who does the coaching or how it occurs, the desire for and benefits of coaching to improve practice and results will persist, because excellent teaching matters to student success.

Preparing to face the inevitable changes is a proactive way to maintain the benefits of coaching, prepare coaches for their new roles, and ensure uninterrupted results.

Scenario

Bill Herrera was a recognized math teacher who wanted to try something different in his work. He loved teaching and had years of experience working with students at all levels of learning mathematics. He also felt challenged by and appreciated the opportunities he had had to mentor novice math teachers and to participate in communities of practice in his school and district. He didn't want to leave a position that offered him direct contact with students, but he wanted to contribute more broadly to education.

A friend who knew and understood Herrera's feelings forwarded him an email announcing an opportunity for experienced math teachers to become online coaches. Herrera laughed at the idea and dismissed the email. A few weeks later, though, his district math coordinator shared a similar announcement in a meeting of all of the district's math teachers. Herrera reconsidered. He completed the online application and went through a rigorous interview process.

He was selected as one of the first 40 national coaches serving in a new program providing technology-mediated personalized coaching to individual teachers. Herrera was excited about the possibilities but still uncertain about his responsibilities. After completing an intensive training program, Herrera was assigned Tuesdays as his coaching day. He logged in at the required time — 4 p.m. to 10 p.m. — checked the coaching platform message box for announcements and new resources posted for coaches' use, visited with other coaches who worked in different parts of the country on the same day, and awaited his first client of the day.

Jennelle Thomas was a new math teacher who had entered teaching through an alternative certification program. She had come from a career in the insurance industry and was extremely knowledgeable about mathematics, but she was having a hard time creating lessons that engaged her students while also managing their behavior. Through the technology platform, Herrera interacted with her by voice and screen share.

As Thomas explained her situation, Herrera listened patiently, asked a few questions, and then helped her focus on a goal that could be achieved during their coaching time. For the remainder of their 45 minutes together, they went to work to help Thomas achieve her goal.

Together they outlined plans for a week's worth of engaging math lessons and discussed ways to assess student learning using a shared document that provided a framework for lesson planning. Through the planning, Herrera modeled what he thought about when planning instruction, coaxed Thomas to think about students who learn differently or are at different levels mathematically, suggested accommodations in the lesson to meet their various needs, and shared resources for both extension and remediation if needed.

Thomas thanked her coach and promised to check in with him the following Tuesday. As he hung up with her, Herrera wondered whether he had done too much for Thomas and began planning his coaching strategies for their next call if she returned for online support and asked to have him coach her again.

In the next call, Herrera decided, he would focus more on helping Thomas understand the research about and basic principles of student engagement, as well as how to incorporate simple strategies into her lesson planning. He believed that he would help Thomas more by developing her foundational knowledge about engagement than if he simply gave her strategies.

Reflection questions

- What prompts teachers to consider serving as a coach? What prompted you or someone you know to become a coach? What reasons for taking on the role might be problematic?

- What are the advantages of coaching online? What are some downsides?

- How might coaches use technology to help coach? How might coaches benefit from using technology?

- How might you approach a coaching session with Thomas? In what ways might your approach have been different than Herrera's?

- What are the pros and cons of Herrera's plan to focus his next call with Thomas on developing her foundational knowledge of the principles and research on engagement? What assumptions was Herrera making?

Recommendations for

Central office administrators

- Emphasize the importance of building leadership capacity among many teachers, not just coaches.
- Develop teacher leaders' facilitation and effective meeting skills.
- Provide professional learning for coaches and teacher leaders to understand the change process, reasons for resistance, and stages of community development.
- Establish a cadre of teacher leaders at each school to collaborate with the coach and school administrators to facilitate and lead change efforts among teacher teams.
- Require that a leadership team made up of teacher leaders guide the school improvement process and carry out the work with their learning teams.
- Explore online resources for coaches and teacher leaders.

Building administrators

- Link coaches' work to student learning goals and school improvement goals.
- Expect coaches to build professional learning communities that have a shared purpose, collaborate, and feel collectively responsible for student success.
- Support the school's emerging and in-practice teacher leaders.
- Create a team of teacher leaders that contributes to professional learning, builds culture, and makes decisions about student achievement.

Coaches

- Support quality instruction by supporting colleagues — co-plan, co-teach, conduct demonstration or model lessons, and observe with feedback.
- Advocate for student achievement.
- Get involved in processes for making decisions that affect school culture.
- Plan and adjust instruction, working in professional learning teams.
- Discuss data to make informed decisions about student learning.
- Create partnerships with families and communities.
- Learn about and get involved in local, state, and national decisions about education.
- Join and become active in district, state or provincial, and national professional organizations.
- Read research about learning to bring the latest knowledge into your practice.

TOOL INDEX
Chapter 14

	TOOL	PURPOSE
14.1	**"Global competence: 10 questions to ask your school/community"**	Answer these questions to guide your school in making decisions that will "bring the world into the classroom."
14.2	**"See me, hear me, coach me"**	Read about using virtual, bug-in-the-ear technology to support real-time coaching.
14.3	**Journey to the future of coaching**	Engage in a visual dialogue about the future of coaching in a team that includes representatives of typical stakeholders, such as coaches, teachers, and principals.
14.4	**Anticipating the future of coaching**	As a design team, anticipate changes in education, teaching, learning, and coaching, and consider how to prepare for those changes.
14.5	**SWOT (strengths, weaknesses, opportunities, and threats) analysis**	This tool provides a process for analyzing the current coaching program and considering what factors might influence it in the future.

To download tools, see www.learningforward.org/publications/coachingmatters

References

Allen, J., Pianta, R., Gregory, A., Mikami, A., & Lun, J. (2011, August). An interaction-based approach to increasing secondary school instruction and student achievement. *Science, 333*(6045), 1034-1037.

Angus, D.L. & Mirel, J.E. (1999). *The failed promise of the American high school.* New York: Teachers College Press.

Atteberry, A. & Bryk, A. (2011, December). Analyzing teacher participation in literacy coaching activities. *The Elementary School Journal, 112*(2), 356-382.

Biancarosa, G., Bryk, A.S., Atteberry, A., & Hough, H. (2010, June). *The impact of literacy coaching on teachers' value-added to student learning in Literacy Collaborative.* Presentation at the Institute of Education Sciences Annual Conference, National Harbor, Maryland, June 28-30, 2010.

Biancarosa, G., Bryk, A.S., & Dexter, E.R. (2010, September). Assessing the value-added effects of Literacy Collaborative professional development on student learning. *The Elementary School Journal, 111*(1), 7-34.

Blasé, J. & Blasé, J. (2006). *Teachers bring out the best in teachers: A guide to peer consultation for administrators and teachers.* Thousand Oaks, CA: Corwin Press.

Borman, J., Feger, S., & Kawakami, N. (2006). *Instructional coaching: Key themes from the literature.* Providence, RI: The Education Alliance Brown University. Available at www.alliance.brown.edu/pubs/pd/TL_Coaching_Lit_Review.pdf.

Brown, D., Reumann-Moore, R., Hugh, R., Christman, J.B., Riffer, M., Plessis, P., & Maluk, H.P. (2007, November). *Making a difference: Year Two report of the Pennsylvania High School Coaching Initiative.* Philadelphia, PA: Research For Action.

Browne, L. (2006). Proposing a proximal principle between peer coaching and staff development as a driver for transformation. *International Journal of Evidence Based Coaching and Mentoring, 4*(1), 31-44.

Bush, R.N. (1984). Effective staff development. In *Making our schools more effective: Proceedings of three state conferences* (pp. 223–238). San Francisco: Far West Laboratory for Educational Research and Development.

Campbell, P. & Malkus, N. (2010). The impact of elementary math specialists. *The Journal of Mathematics and Science: Collaborative Explorations, 12*, 1-28.

Campbell, P. & Malkus, N. (2011, March). The impact of elementary school mathematics coaches on student achievement. *The Elementary School Journal, 111*(3), 430-454.

Costa, A. & Garmston, R. (2002). *Cognitive coaching: A foundation for renaissance schools.* Norwood, MA: Christopher-Gordon.

Creasy, J. & Paterson, F. (2005). *Leading coaching in schools.* Nottingham, United Kingdom: National College for School Leadership.

Crow, T. (Ed.). (2010, May/June). NSDC tools. *Tools for Schools, 13*(4), 4-7.

Curry, M. & Killion, J. (2009, Winter). Slicing the layers of learning: Professional learning communities fill the gaps as educators put new knowledge into practice. *JSD, 30*(1), 56-62.

Danielson, C. (2007). *Enhancing professional practice: A framework for teaching*. Alexandria, VA: ASCD.

Darling-Hammond, L., Wei, R.C., Andree, A., Richardson, N., & Orphanos, S. (2009). *Professional learning in the learning profession: A status report on teacher development in the United States and abroad*. Oxford, OH: NSDC and The School Redesign Network at Stanford University.

Dempsey, N. (2007, Spring). Five elements combine in a formula for coaching: South Carolina initiative carves out time for science and math coaches in schools. *JSD, 28*(2), 10-13.

Elmore, R. (1996). *Bridging the gap between standards and achievement: The imperative for professional development in education*. Washington, DC: The Albert Shanker Institute.

Even, M.J. (1987, June). Why adults learn in different ways. *Lifelong Learning: An Omnibus of Practice and Research, 10*(8), 22-25, 27.

Fairfax County Public Schools. (2008, April). *Cluster-based instructional coaching program: Final evaluation report, 2006-07*. (Available from Fairfax County Public Schools, 8115 Gatehouse Road, Falls Church, VA 22042).

Garet, M., Cronen, S., Eaton, M., Kurki, A., Lugwig., M., Jones, W., et al. (2008, September). *The impact of two professional development interventions on early reading instruction and achievement* (NCEE 2008-4030). Washington, DC: U.S. Department of Education, Institute of Education Sciences, National Center for Education Evaluation and Regional Assistance.

Garet, M., Wayne, A., Stancavage, F., Taylor, J., Walters, K., Song, M., et al. (2010, April). *Middle school mathematics professional development impact study: Findings after the first year of implementation* (NCEE 2010-4009). Washington, DC: U.S. Department of Education, Institute of Education Sciences, National Center for Education Evaluation and Regional Assistance.

Garet, M., Wayne, A., Stancavage, F., Taylor, J., Eaton, M., Walters, K., et al. (2011, May). *Middle school mathematics professional development impact study: Findings after the second year of implementation* (NCEE 2011-4024). Washington, DC: U.S. Department of Education, Institute of Education Sciences, National Center for Education Evaluation and Regional Assistance.

Garmston, R. (1987, February). How administrators support peer coaching. *Educational Leadership, 44*(5), 18-26.

Government of Alberta. (2009, June). Setting the direction framework. Edmonton, Alberta, Canada: Alberta Education. Available at http://education.alberta.ca/media/1082136/sc_settingthedirection_framework.pdf.

Government of Alberta. (2010, November). *Exploring school-based learning coaches in Alberta*. Edmonton, Alberta, Canada: Alberta Education. Available at http://education.alberta.ca/media/6356379/exploringlearningcoaches2010.pdf.

Gutierrez, C. & Bryan, C. (2010, February). An online community becomes a pathway to teacher leadership. *JSD, 31*(1), 42-47.

Guskey, T.R. & Sparks, D. (1996). Exploring the relationship between staff development and improvements in student learning. *Journal of Staff Development, 17*(4), 34-38.

Hall, G. & Hord, S. (2010). *Implementing change: Patterns, principles, and potholes*. Upper Saddle River, NJ: Pearson.

Harrison, C., Clifton, H., & Bryan, C. (2010). *Jeffco Public Schools instructional coach program review*. Golden, CO: Jeffco Public Schools.

Huber, C. (2010, May). Professional learning 2.0. *Educational Leadership, 67*(8), 41-46.

Institute for Educational Leadership. (2001, April). *Leadership for student learning: Redefining the teacher as leader*. Washington, DC: Author.

Ippolito, J. (2009, June 23). *Principals as partners with literacy coaches: Striking a balance between neglect and interference.* Literacy Coaching Clearinghouse. Available at *www.literacycoachingonline.org/briefs/Principals_as_Partners.pdf.*

Jackson, C. & Bruegmann, E. (2009). *Teaching students and teaching each other: The importance of peer learning for teachers.* Cambridge, MA: National Bureau of Economic Research.

Jeffco Public Schools. (2010). Instructional Coach Evaluation Rubric. (Available from Jeffco Public Schools, 1829 Denver West Drive #27, Golden, CO 80401).

Joyce, B. & Showers, B. (1995). *Student achievement through staff development: Fundamentals of school renewal.* White Plains, NY: Longman.

Killion, J. (2012). Coaching in the K-12 context in education. In S. Fletcher & C. McMullen (Eds.), *The Sage handbook of mentoring and coaching* (273-294). London, England: Sage Publications.

Killion, J. & Harrison C. (2006). *Taking the lead: New roles for teachers and school-based coaches.* Oxford, OH: NSDC.

Knight, J. (2004, Spring). Instructional coaches make progress through partnership: Intensive support can improve teaching. *JSD, 25*(2), 32–37.

Knight, J. (2006, April). Instructional coaching: Eight factors for realizing better classroom teaching through support, feedback and intensive, individualized professional learning. *The School Administrator, 63*(4), 36-40.

Knight, J. (2007). *Instructional coaching: A partnership approach to improving instruction.* Thousand Oaks, CA: Corwin Press.

Larner, M. (2007). *Tools for leaders.* New York: Scholastic.

Learning Forward. (2011). *Standards for professional learning.* Oxford, OH: Aut hor.

The Learning Network. (2006). Data sheet: The Learning Network in Battle Creek, MI. Katonah, NY: Richard C. Owen Publishers.

Lucas, T.R. (1999). *Tracking inequality: Stratification and mobility in American high schools.* New York: Teachers College Press.

Mackenzie, N. (Ed.). (2009, April). *A review of the literature.* Setting the Direction Minister's Forum. Alberta, Canada: Alberta Education.

Marsh, J., McCombs, J., Lockwood, J.R., Martorell, F., Gershwin, D., Naftel, S., Le, V., et al. (2008). *Supporting literacy across the sunshine state: A study of Florida middle school reading coaches.* Santa Monica, CA: RAND Corp.

Marzano, R., Pickering, D., & Pollock, J. (2001). *Classroom instruction that works: Research-based strategies for increasing student achievement.* Alexandria, VA: ASCD.

Matsumura, L., Satoris, M., Bickel, D.D., & Garnier, H. (2009). Leadership for literacy coaching: The principal's role in launching a new coaching program. *Educational Administration Quarterly, 45*(5), 655-693.

Moore, R. & Berry, B. (2010, May). The teachers of 2030. *Educational Leadership, 67*(8), 36-40.

Newmann, F.M. & Wehlage, G.G. (1995). *Successful school restructuring.* Madison, WI: Center on Organization and Restructuring of Schools, Wisconsin Center for Education Research.

Poudre School District. (2010). The impact of instructional coaching DVD. (Available from the Poudre School District, 2407 LaPorte Avenue, Fort Collins, CO 80521.)

Reddell, P. (2004, Spring). Coaching can benefit children who have a higher hill to climb. *JSD, 25*(2), 20-26.

Richardson, J. (2008, September). 'Hope is not a strategy': Coaching is effective at closing the gap in Georgia school. *The Learning Principal, 4*(1), 1, 6-7.

Rivera, N., Burley, K., & Sass, J. (2004, February). *Evaluation of school-based professional development (2002-03).* (Los Angeles Unified School District, Planning, Assessment and Research Division Publication No. 187). Available at http://notebook.lausd.net/pls/ptl/url/ITEM/DC60153E2670EBA0E0330A081FB5EBA0.

Rock, M.L., Gregg, M., Howard, P.W., Ploessl, D.M., Maughn, S., et al. (2009, Summer). See me, hear me, coach me. *JSD, 30*(3), 24-32.

Saunders, W., Goldenberg, C., & Gallimore, R. (2009, December). Increasing achievement by focusing grade-level teams on improving classroom learning: A prospective, quasi-experimental study of Title I schools. *American Educational Research Journal, 46*(4), 1006-1033.

Showers, B. (1982, December). *Transfer of training: The contribution of coaching.* Eugene, OR: University of Oregon, College of Education, Center for Educational Policy and Management.

Showers, B. (1984, October). *Peer coaching: A strategy for facilitating transfer of training.* Eugene, OR: University of Oregon, College of Education, Center for Educational Policy and Management.

Shulman, L.S. (1998). Theory, practice, and the education of professionals. *The Elementary School Journal, 98*(5), 511-526.

South Carolina's Coalition for Math & Science. (2008). *iCoaching: Student achievement analysis 2008.* Clemson, SC: Author.

Sparks, D. (2005). *Leading for results.* Thousand Oaks, CA: Corwin Press.

Sumner, K. (2011). *An explanatory mixed-methods study of instructional coaching practices and their relationship to student achievement.* Unpublished dissertation, Western Carolina University, Cullowhee, NC.

Sweeny, B. (2001). *Leading the teacher induction and mentoring program.* Thousand Oaks, CA: Corwin Press.

Taylor, M.J. (2008). *Instructional support for teachers: An evaluation of professional development and instructional coaching (in SB185 consortium and site funded schools).* Littleton, CO: MJT Associates.

Teacher Leader Standards Exploratory Consortium. (2011). *Teacher leader model standards.* Princeton, NJ: ETS. Available at www.teacherleaderstandards.org/downloads/TLS_Brochure.pdf.

Teachstone Training. (2012). *The CLASS tool.* Charlottesville, VA: Author. Available at www.teachstone.org/about-the-class.

The Learning Network. (2006). Data sheet: The Learning Network in Battle Creek, Mich. Katonah, NY: Richard C. Owen Publishers.

Thornton, C. (2010). *Group and team coaching: The essential guide.* London: Routledge.

Truesdale, W. (2003). *The implementation of peer coaching on the transferability of staff development to classroom practice in two selected Chicago public elementary schools.* Chicago: Loyola University.

Valencia, S. & Killion, J. (1988, Spring). Overcoming obstacles to teacher change: Directions from school-based efforts. *Journal of Staff Development, 9*(2), 168-174.

Vervago Inc. (2009). *Precision Q & A workshop fact sheet.* Available at www.vervago.com/PQFactSheet.pdf.

West, L. (2009). Content coaching: Transforming the teaching profession. In J. Knight (Ed.), *Coaching: Approaches and perspectives* (pp. 113-144). Thousand Oaks, CA: Corwin Press.

Wren, S. & Vallejo, D. (2009). *Effective collaboration between instructional coaches and principals.* Available at www.balancedreading.com/Wren_&_Vallejo_Coach_Principal_Relationships.pdf.

York-Barr, J. & Duke, K. (2004, Fall). What do we know about teacher leadership? Findings from two decades of scholarship. *Review of Educational Research, 74*(3), 255-316.

Acknowledgments

Throughout our experiences working with coaches, in some cases for more than 25 years, we have appreciated the depth of passion, committed purpose, and gritty tenacity of coaches who work in schools to strengthen teaching and learning and build a collaborative culture that allows everyone in school to learn and grow each day. We would not know what we do without the opportunity to work side by side with these coaches, their principals, central office champions, and state and provincial leaders who believe in the potential of continuous, school-based professional learning as the foundation for increased student achievement.

We would easily fill an entire volume with the names of coaches who have been our teachers. The idea for this book on coaching emerged from our extended work in coaching over nearly two decades and from the evaluation of the instructional coaching program in Jeffco (Jefferson County, Colo.) Public Schools, that Cindy Harrison, Chris Bryan, and Heather Clifton did. As a result of this work, we became clearer about what makes coaching effective and what districts, schools, coach champions, and coaches do to ensure that coaching results in increased student learning. Through the years, we have had the opportunity to shape and influence coaching programs in many schools and school systems in the United States and Canada. Each opportunity, whether it was a short-term or multi-year experience, influenced how we think about the important work coaches do each day.

This book is possible because, individually and collectively, many have been and continue to be our coaches and teachers. We acknowledge that what we know and do is informed by researchers and practitioners who work with us in the field of professional learning, and coaching in particular. We are grateful that we benefit from our ongoing collaboration with each other and value having a team of committed colleagues who share one another's values, challenge each other's assumptions, and push each of us to achieve more than we can individually. Lastly, we express our appreciation to our families who provide the emotional support and give us the space and time to devote to our work.

About the authors

Joellen Killion is a senior adviser with Learning Forward and a senior consultant with Learning Forward Center for Results. As senior adviser at Learning Forward, Killion leads initiatives related to examining the link between professional development and student learning. She has extensive experience in planning, design, implementation, and evaluation of professional development at the school, system, and state/provincial level. She has conducted evaluations of projects funded by federal and private foundation grants. She led the recent revision of the Standards for Professional Learning and the Innovation Configuration maps.

Killion has 40 years of experience as a leader in professional learning and provides professional learning services to schools, districts, and governmental education agencies around the world. Killion also has served as Learning Forward's deputy executive director, directed Learning Forward's Academy and Coaches Academy programs, and facilitated multiple grant-funded initiatives. She has held positions as a teacher, teacher leader, curriculum director, school administrator in school districts in Colorado and as a teacher in Michigan. She served on Learning Forward's Board of Trustees for six years and as its president. Killion is co-author with Pat Roy of *Becoming a Learning School* (NSDC, 2009), with Stephanie Hirsh of *The Learning Educator: A New Era for Professional Learning* (NSDC, 2007), and with Cindy Harrison of *Taking the Lead: New Roles for Teachers and School-Based Coaches* (NSDC, 2006). In addition, she is the author of *Assessing Impact: Evaluating Staff Development*, 2nd ed. (NSDC & Corwin Press, 2008) and numerous articles, papers, reports, books, and presentation manuals. Her scholarly writing focuses on evaluating professional learning, research-based practices in professional learning, and coaching.

Cindy Harrison is an international educational consultant in instructional coaching, leadership, organizational change, and professional learning. Harrison consults with school districts, professional groups and organizations throughout the world providing training and on-site services in creating instructional coaching programs, teacher leader programs and evaluation systems for principals and teachers. She has been a consultant and presenter to organizations including the Association for Supervision and Curriculum Development (ASCD), the National Staff Development Council (NSDC), the Colorado Principals' Center, educational

services centers, businesses, and various types of school districts. Currently, she is working with state agencies and districts implementing the Common Core State Standards.

Harrison served as director of staff development in a large suburban school district with 32,000 students and 42 school sites for 27 years, designing and delivering a variety of professional learning programs for administrators, teachers, and classified staff.

She has been a middle school principal, teacher at all secondary levels, a curriculum writer and a central office director. She has served as president of NSDC (now Learning Forward), as well as the Colorado Staff Development Council. She has written training manuals and co-authored the ASCD videotape series on shared decision making and conflict resolution. Her articles have appeared in *Educational Leadership*, the *Journal of Staff Development*, and *The Developer*. She is co-author with Joellen Killion of *Taking the Lead: New Roles for Teachers and School-Based Coaches* (NSDC, 2006).

Chris Bryan is a senior consultant with the Learning Forward Center for Results and an international consultant for school-based coaches in differentiated instruction and school improvement.

Through the Center for Strategic Quality Professional Development, she has supported and facilitated schools' work to build and sustain change.

Bryan has more than three decades of experience in education as a classroom teacher, learning specialist, mentor, staff developer, instructional coach, coach of coaches, and in university partnership programs. She teaches and supervises student teachers at the University of Colorado Health Sciences Center and is an executive coach for principals for Denver Public Schools.

Bryan is co-developer of the six-day Learning Forward Coaches Academy and of advanced coaching modules offered through Learning Forward's Center for Results. With Learning Forward's Colorado affiliate, she co-designed and co-taught a School Leadership Institute as part of a School Leadership Academy in partnership with the St. Vrain Valley (Colo.) School District.

She is a frequent presenter at the Tointon Institute for Educational Change Summer Conference in Vail, Colo. She is past president of Learning Forward's Colorado affiliate and a current member of the Affiliate Leadership Committee. Her articles have been published in *JSD*.

Heather Clifton is a professional learning consultant for schools, districts, state and municipal agencies, and nonprofit organizations in many aspects of professional development and organizational reform. She has provided executive coaching to school principals and teachers at all levels and has facilitated the work of district and school leadership teams. She offers training and support for instructional coaches and their principals. She has taught university classes and has experience as a teacher, elementary school principal, and central office curriculum and staff development specialist.

She is a co-developer of training modules for Learning Forward's Coaches Academy, assisted in the design and delivery of the teacher leadership certification program with the Front Range Board of Cooperative Educational Services and the University of Colorado–Denver, and was a facilitator of the Community Learning Network, a project of the Annie E. Casey Foundation. She also served as co-president of the Colorado Staff Development Council.